The FAX CLUB Experiment...

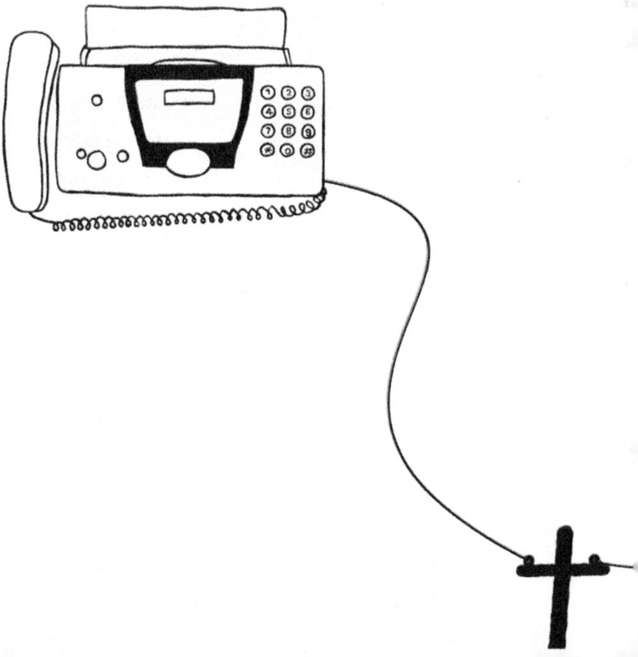

PRAISE FOR THIS BOOK

"In a world obsessed with certainty and speed, The Fax Club Experiment honours something more powerful: the transformational space that opens up when we ask better questions, and dare to sit with them. This book is a powerful reminder that the deepest insights don't come from answers, but from the courage to wonder differently. For coaches, leaders, and anyone committed to growth."

KAREN KIMSEY-HOUSE
Co-founder, The Co-Active Training Institute

"The Fax Club Experiment reveals something many of us know inherently to be true, but struggle to admit: we don't need more technology to live more connected lives, we need less. By stripping back to an obsolete method of communication, 100 strangers were able to cut through our modern noise to reveal profound wisdom, authenticity, vulnerability, and true human potential. This experiment shows just how urgently we must assess which aspects of our digital age are beneficial, and which are actually counterintuitive to our flourishing. Sometimes the only way forward is to look to the past."

KATE ROBINSON
Sir Ken Robinson Foundation, Author of *Imagine If...*

The FAX CLUB Experiment...

A crazy idea.

It shouldn't have worked.

But it did.

Written by The 32

The Fax Club Experiment by The 32

Published by The Fax Club Press

TheFaxClubExperiment.com

Cover by The Fax Club Press

ISBN: 978-1-0369-3307-4

Printed in United Kingdom

1st Edition

This book is printed on demand, which reduces supply chain waste, greenhouse emissions, and conserves valuable natural resources.

The purpose of print-on-demand book manufacturing, is to reduce our environmental impact. Traditional offset printing usually requires large orders in anticipation of sales. Often, any books that go unsold are destroyed. This results in wasted paper, wasted energy, added greenhouse emissions, pulping, and landfill overflows.

This book is dedicated to the non-conformists,
to everyone who dares to be, think and do differently.

Welcome to Fax Club.

1. The first rule of Fax Club:
   You do not talk about Fax Club.
2. The second rule of Fax Club:
   You DO NOT talk about Fax Club.
3. The third rule of Fax Club:
   We do not follow.

FOREWORD

There's a moment when someone decides to care again.
It can be quiet, almost invisible.

About their words. About their thoughts. About the questions they haven't asked in far too long. That's what this book is about.

When we started Fax Club, it was a hunch.

A slightly mad idea in a world obsessed with speed: what if we slowed down and thought deeply, once a week?

What if 100 strangers agreed to wrestle with one good question at a time, not to win, but to discover something new in themselves?

We didn't know how it would go.

What happened over the following 52 weeks was a kind of magic.
Not the loud kind. The quiet, creeping kind that stays with you.
These weren't just answers. They were confessions. Manifestos.
Memos to a future self. Love letters to lost versions.
Quiet revolutions.

Everyone wrote. No names, just numbers. But somehow, the truth rang louder than ever.

This book is the best of that year. A paper trail of soul-searching and side-stepping the obvious. It's proof that people still want to go deep. Still want to think. Still want to feel something real.

If you hold this book in your hands, read slowly. Let it ask you questions back.

Because that's the point of a good question, it doesn't close a conversation. It opens one.

Stay curious,

David Hieatt

Co-founder of The DO Lectures and creator of Fax Club

Contents

Introduction 1
How to use this book 3
1. The 3-hour work day 4
2. The community that never meets 8
3. The business you never sell 11
4. Customers run your business 14
Why did you join Fax Club? 17
5. Rewarding failure 20
6. A book for life 22
7. The big ask 25
8. Discount day 28
Why did you choose your Fax Club number? 32
9. A tale of two letters 34
10. Sociable media 38
11. Rock around the clock 41
12. The richest person no one knows 45
How did you get hold of your fax machine? 48
13. Let them in 49
14. Tiny pieces of grit 51
15. Rules to live by 53
16. The currency of contentment 57
What did being a member of Fax Club teach you? 60
17. Comedic timing 63
18. It's your funeral 66
19. Stubborn as donkeys 70
20. We don't talk about Fax Club 73
What was it like being anonymous? 75
21. Two minutes in the here and now 78
22. Short-term dumb. Long-term smart. 80
23. People change people 83
24. Problem hunters 85
What kept you here if you wobbled? 90
25. A letter to the boss 92
26. Five years of happy 98

27. The reverse bucket list 102
28. Small talk, big truths 105
What was it like to finally meet in person? 108
29. Blow the budget 110
30. The book that will change your life 114
31. Order some magnitude 116
32. A good job, according to Breslin 119
What has it been like producing this book? 124
33. The robots have arrived 126
34. Stop. Stop. Stop. 130
35. The Brain Trust 133
36. White lies 136
Is life after Fax Club any different? 138
37. Silence has the answer 140
38. The pleasure paradox 142
39. Reverse-engineering success 146
40. The Solomon Paradox 148
41. The curiosity budget 151
42. Truths we don't agree on 153
What does Fax Club mean to you in three words? 155
43. Walk in their shoes 156
44. My chemical gratitude 160
45. The year of nothing new 164
46. The thorn in your side 166
Did you follow the rules? 170
47. Shared beliefs, shared limitations 172
48. Small experiment, big idea 175
49. More fool us 178
50. Building different 182
51. The questions that made you truly think 186
52. What's your question? 189
The end... or the beginning? 191
About the authors 192
Acknowledgements 193

Question 1
What would have to happen for this to be true? You only work three hours a day and yet your business still grows?

Introduction

We are Fax Club.

A year-long experiment in counterintuitive thinking and community building.

The concept was simple:

- 52 weeks
- 52 questions
- 100 mavericks
- 1 anonymous community

Every Friday, a single question arrived by fax. (Yes, you needed a fax machine.)

It was hard to join and even harder to stay. If you joined Fax Club, you couldn't tell anyone or reveal your name. We were anonymous to each other, known only by a number.

Each week we shared our answers with the 99 other numbers on an online forum. Modern technology mixed with analogue fax. Word limits were honoured and ignored in equal measure. We voted on the answers we liked the best, the counterintuitive ones, the ones that spoke to us. And then we began replying to posts. Conversations sparked up. Connection grew. Intimacy invited.

The platform changed. Some people dropped out and some were dropped. A quiet community arose, united in our anonymity and connected by our stories.

A year later, 32 of us completed the experiment. Stubborn, persistent, call us what you will. Only then did we meet in person for the first time. In a room full of strangers, we knew intimate and personal stories about each other, just not who owned which story.

And in this meeting of collaborators was a further invitation. Another question. "If a room of strangers were to write a book, how would they do it?"

This is our book of the fax club questions and selected answers. It captures the most powerful moments and revelations from 52 weeks of radical curiosity. Snapshots of real people, real lives. Each answer a new possibility.

And while answers are useful and necessary, it seems that somewhere along the line humanity has shifted to prioritising having answers over asking questions.

We educate, then test our children on their ability to learn the correct answer. We reward and promote workers for their ability to find answers.

But correct answers are seldom interesting. Like asking, "How is that magic trick done?", only to have the magic fade in the telling.

Questions, on the other hand, are powerful and stimulating. The best answer is often just the next better question, expanding the conversation and inviting diverse thinking. Better questions are always interesting.

Wrestling with questions, looking at them sideways, grows creativity, adaptability, innovation, deeper understanding, greater ease, resilience, more fun and importantly, self-discovery.

This book of answers is itself an answer to the questions we asked of ourselves along the way:

- "How can we create a community when people are anonymous and can never meet?"
- "What's the antidote to a disconnected world driven by on-demand consumption?"
- "How does anonymity impact building intimacy?"
- "Can we do what we said we set out to do?"

We humans are meaning-making machines. We search for meaning in everything. Asking questions is how we make sense of our experience.

Fax Club created insight.

The episodic nature of our commitment to each other created structure and certainty. Anonymity invited courageous disclosure and straight-talking.

The questions engaged us. Our answers created relationships and intimacy. Our arguments and disagreements built trust. Our conversations invited curiosity and listening.

The faxes invoked nostalgia for a slower, simpler past of more connection. Patience, appreciation and excitement for the next chapter. Anticipation of what comes next.

In sharing our stories, we grew closer. We inspired one another and created hope for a better future.

If you're reading this, we did it. We spent a year writing together and then published a book. We did what we said we set out to do. And now you're part of it.

How to use this book

This book can be read from front to back, or opened at random and read question by question. Much like the original participants, you can devour every word, asking yourself how you might answer, or you can select just the parts that light some kind of spark.

All the questions we answered as a group are included. You will like some better than others. Likewise the answers.

You will also get to meet us, the community of strangers who contributed not only the answers, but ensured this experiment found its way into the written form you're reading now.

We hope it inspires you to take the time to answer questions, and ask bigger ones.

Question 1

The 3-hour work day

What would have to happen for this to be true: you only work three hours a day and yet your business still grows?

#25:

This comes down to how we define 'growth'.

Everywhere you look, you're told that bigger is better; that growth is the ultimate barometer of progress. But doesn't this just end up distracting us from what truly matters?

Growing isn't inherently bad, but too often growth can end up as a vanity metric, with true value (or 'success' as we call it) found in the margins.

My business is not so much about how big I can become, but how meaningful I can be. My growth aligns with my purpose, so I'd spend three hours focused on making that a reality and cut out the rest.

Sometimes, the most powerful move is to zig when the whole world zags. Easy... right?

#103:

Fold my business.

Yes! I am going to do it. I will be more creative, more productive, and have more money (because I will have less outgoings to spend on stock purchasing). It's so simple and I've only just seen it.

#06:

Fire clients, raise fees.

1. **I fire 70% of my existing clients**
   The ones that aren't really MY people. The ones that aren't playing ALL-IN on stuff that's truly IMPORTANT to them; that don't excite me.
2. **Expand into the space**
   This creates space and energy to show up more powerfully for the clients I truly love, EVOKING greater TRANSFORMATION within them. When they create bigger impact then word-of-mouth referrals grow.
3. **I increase my fees**
   In working with fewer people, who are creating more meaningful change, the value of what they create in their lives grows, and so does what they pay me for that value.
4. **Give myself away**
   Now I've created the life where I get to be generous with everything, to everyone.

To summarise, reduce hours by firing clients, keeping only those who are truly creating from their essence, creating the biggest value, and raising my fees because that still represents significant ROI for them.

#11:

Option 1: If you make your work you, you are the brand…
then you can just be yourself and your business will grow.
The ultimate influencer.

Option 2: Give away 49% of your business to 49 individuals (at 1% each) who you believe are hungry for success and have the drive to make it happen, and there's a chance at least one of them will come up trumps.

#12:

To make this truly work the rule needs to apply for **everyone**. We collectively re-envision the way we view time spent on work and **grow our businesses, communities, society and our economy together.**

- Everyone works **three hours a day.**
- Everyone must also work or volunteer **one additional hour a day in a contrarian job to their 'usual' one**. E.g. Execs look after the children in childcare. Roadworks workers teach an art class. Uni students work at the retirement home. Chefs work as firefighters.
- Everyone has the **option to take on a second 'bonus' 3-hour a day job**, not for financial reasons but for the **enjoyment, growth, or connection** the role will bring them.
- All organisations require those working for them to have **one hour a day synchronised**. The other hours can be worked whenever the individual chooses.

The net result would be all organisations have a much larger workforce with diverse backgrounds leading to more creative thinking and most likely more efficiencies, whilst at the same time everyone gets to work less.

What would schools look like?

All schools would require pupils and staff to synchronise a one-hour focused learning session a day.

For the rest of the day teachers (and non-teachers) can create lessons (a max of two hours per day each) and pupils follow interest-directed learning, attending the classes that draw their attention.

What would hospitals look like?

Doctors use their three hours to fully focus on their jobs. The extended workforce who then choose to spend their time supporting hospitals pick up the admin and the human side, e.g. spending time just chatting with patients.

For certain roles that may require longer than three hours a day, such as a surgeon, they can 'stack' their hours. Doing six in one day. The next day they can spend doing a contrarian role such as tending the garden at their local park.

Optimising societal time spent on work

We commission a cross-disciplined team of academics to build an AI model that when programmed with personal and societal KPIs (e.g. environment, profit, health, happiness, connection) will recommend the optimal deployment of the collective workforce hours. The goal is to stop spending our time working on things that aren't serving us as a society or as individuals.

One week a year we play work hours Uno

During Uno week you get to 'draw' one Uno work card a day. If you get a wild card 'you can swap work hours with someone else', 'clear your work hours for that week', 'add four more hours to your week'.

Question 2

The community that never meets

Fellow faxers,

We did the first question. We learnt a bunch. It was a little messy, but we will make it a little smoother as we go. Remember, we are trying something new, that is what makes this so exciting.

Reading the answers, it became apparent something amazing is happening here.

Now, the question this week is about community:

How do we bring a community together, even if they can never meet, with one simple counterintuitive act?

#80:

I had two ideas.

First up, the more emotional idea: we all ask for help, and then freely give it where we can.

Why it matters?

Helping someone doesn't just create an obligation from the recipient to the giver, it also creates a paternalistic (for want of a better word. A sense of concern and wish for their well being) bond from the giver about the recipient.

If we help someone, we feel closer to them.

Ask for help, because you know what's most valuable to you right now (even if that's clarity on what help you need) and because it's often obscure to people that the skill or resource they have could be useful to others.

Second, my more practical/physical idea: we arrange small Fika-like meetings of just a few people, but rotating around.

Why?

It's hard to get to know one another as a big blob. Smaller chats will make sure everyone's voice gets heard, and create opportunities for lots of little one-to-one connections to form. That's where the power of community lies.

We'll have to rotate around so that we get the chance to chat with everyone.

Perhaps we could gamify it a little, like trying to catch all the Pokémon?

#103:

I don't believe it's possible to form a true community without in-person meetings.

So much of how we connect with other people is to do with body language, inference, tone, eye contact. It's a basic need. Anything else is just dopamine driven. I think this is why we get social media fatigue.

So my answer would be that in order to bring a community together, you would need a small amount of investment involved (e.g. a fax machine!) and a new angle. People will always activate themselves for this.

"Bring an odd (clean) sock and we'll try and match it with someone else's."

What better excuse to meet? People need close human connection.

#71:

At the start of this experiment, each member of the community gets sent a packet of seeds 🌱

On the front:

> Plant these seeds, and watch them grow.
> As your shoots unfurl, they are unfurling alongside others.
> You are part of something, the cycle of life itself.
> You are part of the world's experiment.
> You are growing, alongside other humans.
> You made something grow, together.
> How much more can you grow, now?
> What seeds will you plant together, next?

"If a world is dreamable, maybe it can be dreamed into being."
David Mitchell, *Cloud Atlas*

Question 3

The business you never sell

If you could never sell your business, how would you build it differently?

#25:

The very premise of the question assumes that the ultimate goal of creating the business in the first instance is to sell it. However, this comes with its own challenges, placing greater worth on the short-term "perceived value", i.e. what people (investors) see as the number of zeros after the $ sign, over the often softer, intrinsic investment made in the people and culture.

I'm actually in the process of exploring how to build employee co-ownership into my business that matures over time up to their retirement, intertwining employees' futures with company success.

This does three things simultaneously:

1. It cultivates an ecosystem in which people feel valued rather than a cog in a larger wheel.
2. It creates a sense of security, incentivising employees to see work as a longer-term legacy rather than "just another job".
3. It redefines what success is, shifting away from exit strategies or acquisition offers towards the depth of commitment and strength of the collective.

I'm personally more interested in building something that is a testament to the belief that the true value of a business lies not in its price tag but in the purpose it serves and the community it sustains.

#71:

When I started out on my own six years ago, I felt ill whenever I heard the term "lifestyle business". Guilty. Fake. Like an impostor.

Now I think, why is that an insult?!

If I'm never selling my business, **then I'm never selling control**. I'm not ruled by ego, or making money for other shareholders, or growth for growth's sake.

I can do the work myself - instead of creating a machine to do the work, leaving me just an operator, feeding the machine.

I can break the rules - trust my instinct, be opportunistic, follow my heart.

I can spend the profits - reinvest it my own learning, my customers, my community, my planet.

I can live in the moment - it's not about building assets, or a "brand identity", or an "employee experience". It's just me, working with people I love, doing the work I love, for people I love.

A Livelihood Business.

I'm here for a good time, not for a long time ✌️

#101:

If you could never sell your business, how would you build it differently?

Community, Sustainability and Legacy through:

- Creating a long term vision over short term goals
- Building an exceptional culture
- Focus on community and environment impact
- Embedding continuous adaptation and innovation
- Developing long lasting customer relationships
- Establishing a positive succession structure
- Aligning with personal values and passions

#06:

My business is built on 1:1 relationships as a service business. There's nothing here of value to be sold on.

In order for this work that I do to engage and fulfil me, it will have to sustain me through the rest of my life. It's not work. It's how I choose to spend my time.

I am metaphorically going rock-climbing in the mountains every time I work with a client. It's how I want to live.

Given this, a couple of realisations come to me...

- I want to be doing this for a long time
- I need to create a path toward mastery (prioritise learning)
- I want to share the wisdom and the value my clients create for themselves with others
- I need to do my own work, to care for myself, to sustain myself
- I should double down on asking for help

Question 4

Customers run your business

If your customers run your business for a month, what is the one new product or service that they would launch?

And how do you know?

#50:

My clients want a product that allows them to speed up time. To get through the hard stuff, without getting through the hard stuff. A jump to the happy ending, or at least to the less-painful middle. What I'm selling, really, is help tolerating the present. And the third option here (the counterintuitive solution to the problem of suffering?): to slow time, or at least expand the difficult-now. I think there's something to that. The client wants to hurry along, let's get this over with, but the product they need is "the relisher." The thing that allows us to honor the horrible, the violent, the ugly, in such a way that we lose fear of all possible future torments.

#26:

My customers are patients. Operation dates are "within the next six months" and patients can't plan their lives. The result: a digital countdown waiting list relevant for operations.

#20:

They would launch a bring-back scheme or recycling/reuse hub. How do I know? Because they share my values ♥.

#18:

If my customers had the reins for a month, they'd have a disruptive, boundary-pushing platform (maybe boundary-less) with unlimited access to me non-stop for interaction, and they would want create something that that challenges the status quo. It's all about innovation, creativity, and making a statement. They want to shake things up and create something that's never been seen before.

How do I know? Because they're drawn to the brand for its boldness, its refusal to conform, its vision. They see the future in what we do to confront norms, and they want in on crafting that future. It's in the feedback, the engagement, the way they push for more. It's clear they're not just looking for the next big thing; they want to be the next big thing.

#15:

My business is young and our clients haven't yet had the opportunity to meet. By virtue of investing in our solution, they are all like-minded souls and would enjoy the opportunity to get together. I suspect they'd organise an informal annual gathering without a specific agenda. An opportunity to get to know each other better and cross-pollinate ideas outside the direct scope of our business. I'd like to provide that opportunity soon.

#32:

So in my business the customers would sell their knowledge and expertise to promote the fact that everybody's experience is valuable, should be recognised and taken into consideration. These people should be found in the most unlikely places and perhaps shouldn't even be existing customers. Considering AI, it is concerning that many products we find today have not been designed by the end users. For example many products intended for women have been designed for men and this is an issue with the difference between designers and end users.

The effect of this would be a closer society where everyone can contribute something meaningful and be part of creating the future world. Unfortunately at the moment we have a system where a few design and create the future however we all live in it (not only gender-wise).

The book *Invisible Women* by Caroline Criado Perez talks about this further and how certain products such as seat belts have been designed by men, as well as the design of cities. These examples demonstrate the topic from a gender perspective however this can be applied to many different aspects, I think the key here is to place value on the end user and encourage them to contribute to the products they use and be an integral part of the development process so the products are not developed in a silo.

#88:

They'd launch clarity, because that's what they're really buying.

#06:

I fancy they'd launch their own mastermind community. A fee-based (commitment-based) membership of course.

My clients in leadership are 1:1. Many have commonalities in the value they discover in our work together:

- a trusted, objective, outsider with no skin in the game
- a sense of being witnessed, that counters the loneliness they feel in their role
- creates collaboration and co-creation
- someone that sees what others do not
- having someone say what others will not say

I sense there's a yearning for more belonging and community.
A small group space that is high-commitment and high-intimacy.
A place where (self) work gets done.
The small gathering balances diversity with similarity. Just the right amount of "Q"[1] as a measure of social connectivity and familiarity.

Hmm. How come I'm not doing this yet?

---

1 Uzzi, Brian (September 2005). "Collaboration and Creativity: The Small World Problem". American Journal of Sociology.

Meet the members of Fax Club

Why did you join Fax Club?

#95:

My Dad's fax machine had sat in the attic since 2016, the year he died of Parkinson's. Forms of communication that don't rely on speech become vital in times of such illness. I imagined his face lighting up as it whirred back to life! When it didn't work, my heart sank.

Having read Jem Bendell's essay "Deep Adaptation", I wondered if the lowly fax could pulse back to life during a major digital shutdown. My curiosity was stoked!

#74:

To change my mind.

Get things done. With other doers. Over 52 weeks.

With a different way of thinking. Counterintuitive, they call it.

It was a way for me to confirm the incredible power of (crazy) ideas.

#50:

I just remember how I felt reading that first Fax Club email. Of course there are many things I don't have control over (of course!), but my life feels very controlled, very ordinary. I have my little morning routine, my work routine, my evening routine. Even when these are going well, they can feel painfully... familiar. But Fax Club! Fax Club was a WILD idea, and I knew only others interested in wild ideas would join. I had no idea what would happen next, and that was entirely the appeal.

#71:

I was feeling a bit professionally lonely: working on my own, lacking a tribe. I was drawn to both the writing element and the participation ritual of something that felt challenging and rewarding. I'm very curious, and I love experiments. Also, I loved the idea of having something secret that was just mine to work on and play with. Plus I used to fax my best friend and my boyfriend when I was a teenager (and it was definitely not normal).

#25:

Because I'm a sucker for an experiment, especially one that promises to stretch my thinking. Also, because it was cryptic, and the best things in life - treasure maps, secret societies, and why people still order espresso martinis - usually are.

#98:

Because I knew it would take effort. Effort that others wouldn't be able to commit to.

And effort that would make me part of something forever.
A collective that had taken the personal decision to do something different. To be part of a story that could be passed from generation to generation.

Ultimately, I knew it would bring me joy.

#48:

It was a leap of faith at a time when I knew I needed to be braver. I've found it hard to be consistent with certain things in my life, especially if they are non-essential, and I knew Fax Club would both challenge and enrich my life. Also, who doesn't want to join a club with 100 other people who would see an opportunity like this and think 'I'm in!' I knew I needed more people like that around me.

#06:

It was a glorious experiment and perfect vehicle to double down on creating a writing practice, getting opinionated and moving past perfectionism. Fax Club is an invitation to intentionally engage in life, to commit to the future and to show up.

#38:

I was at a low point and this built up my confidence and helped me reconnect with ideas bigger than myself. It saved my life.

#78:

When I read the post, I just knew I wanted in, I can't explain it, something pulled me in! So it became more a "why not". I like to challenge myself and this sounded unique, yet a bit unknown. I wasn't sure how it would work, you had to work it out as you went. Things weren't always how I expected and I just rolled with it.

#102:

Why wouldn't I join Fax Club? There were hardly any reasons not to. I work in an environment where most people think alike; creativity and out-of-the-box thinking aren't exactly the norm. I wanted to be inspired, to surround myself with fresh ideas rather than always having to generate them on my own. And beyond that, there was something almost magical about it, an energy I knew I didn't want to miss out on.

Question 5

Rewarding failure

How would you create a culture of creativity where people were not afraid of failure?

E.g. An awards night where the prizes go to the biggest failures.

#71:

In the garden culture, ideas or projects have one of three statuses:

(1) Seedling 🌱

When a project is a seedling, no negative judgement or alternative suggestions may be offered by anyone. The idea must ONLY receive encouragement and space to grow, and the only person allowed to alter it is the originator. Seedlings are kept in the greenhouse and no one can stamp on them.

(2) Bud 🌿

When the originator is ready, the project is moved to the budding stage. No encouragement is offered, everyone who comes into contact with it must try their best to kill it. Everyone should behave as an adverse weather event: test it, freeze it, blow it over. The originator's job is to listen, not to defend. Looping back to the seedling stage for reformulation is expected.

(3) Mature Shrub 🪴

When the originator is satisfied, the project moves to maturity and is either implemented straight away or planted in the garden to be harvested later.

In this growth culture, failure is deliberate, at the right stage of development. It must happen to everyone, it's not wielded as a weapon, but as a tool for cultivation 🌳

#102:

One failure project per year.

Every year we write up our goals for the year. They're supposed to be ambitious but achievable and if we achieve all of them we did well that year. Nobody wants to fail. But nobody is creative or tries something outside of the box for fear of failure.

The idea here is to have a few goals every year that are set up for possible failure. At the end of year you must have failed at least on one project. If you haven't that means you've played it too safe. You'll still have your typical goals and things where you get to feel good about typical success. But by making failure more normal we become more creative and hopefully it won't just stay with one goal per year but you in time you'll be comfortable to fail fast and often but are still productive in the long run.

#25:

I'm proposing "Anti-Goals", turning conventional goal-setting on its head by focusing on what we wish to avoid as well as achieve.

Our culture is obsessed with success, yet I don't know anyone who can actually say what that means. Anti-Goals offer a reflective counterbalance, prompting the identification and articulation of the most undesirable outcomes to help foster creativity.

They also help clarify what success does not look like. Mitigating fear of failure by making it a conscious, navigable part of the planning process. Placing equal value on understanding what to avoid as well as the end destination.

Question 6

A book for life

You can only read one book (as many times as you'd like) for the rest of your life.

What would it be and why?

#24:

If I had to choose one book to read for the rest of my life, it would be a blank notebook. My choice defies conventional expectations of choosing a book filled with content to consume. My blank notebook, a canvas for creativity and introspection, becomes a living document of personal evolution. It offers an infinite playground for my thoughts, stories, and reflections, making it the most dynamic and personalised book possible. Unlike traditional books, a blank notebook grows with you, the pages a testament to a journey of self-expression and discovery. I'd choose it.

#74:

The Man who Planted Trees by Jean Giono

French author. Fresh ideas.

It's a tale about a man who planted trees.

One by one. All year long. During decades.

Hundreds and hundreds. Of all sorts.

Many died, but most survived. In the mid of the 20th century, this story was all about patience, commitment, determination and impact.

So modern. So wise. So provoking.

Why are we so slow to understand that the power of one can change the lives of thousands?

A few pages before the end of the story:

“Everything was changed. Even the air. Instead of the harsh dry winds that used to attack me, a gentle breeze was blowing, laden with scents. A sound like water came from the mountains: it was the wind in the forest. Most amazing of all, I heard the actual sound of water falling into a pool. I saw that a fountain had been built, that it flowed freely and–what touched me most-that someone had planted a linden beside it, a linden that must have been four years old, already in full leaf, the incontestable symbol of resurrection.”

Move your body, get to the bookshop, buy one. Or two.

One for you and your kids. Another one for your neighbour, colleague, bus driver...

We’ll build our future.

Together.

One tree after the other.
One page after the other.
One idea at a time.
One breath... until the last.

That's life!

#13:

FAX CLUB

RECIPIENTS: #00–#107

SENDER: #13

SUBJECT: Fax#6

MESSAGE:

Q:
If you could only read one book (as many times as you'd like) for the rest of your life. What would it be and why?

A:
The Daily Stoic by Ryan Holiday
A collection of classic wisdom from Stoic Philosophers.
Delivered in easily digestible segments.
One lesson a day for an entire year.
Learn how to achieve clarity, serenity and resilience.
Use them to become the best person you can be.
Make it an habitual lifelong practice.

LOVE #13

Question 7

The big ask

We need to get better at asking. What is the one ask that you have been putting off for ages and why?

#12:

Standing in line at a coffee shop on Saturday morning I noticed a man two people ahead of me. He had the appearance of being homeless. I watched as he ordered his coffee. I had already decided that I would pay for it… but, I hesitated to speak up.

I watched as the barista brewed his coffee and requested the £3.95 payment. I watched as the man fumbled in his pockets, his eyes darting around the coffee shop, his face full of shame. Before he could ask I found my voice and offered to pay.

This got me thinking. Whilst we do need to get better at asking, we also need to get better at giving.

A friend founded a movement 11 years ago called Suspended Coffees. Suspended Coffees aimed to preempt the 'ask' by encouraging customers to pay in advance for a coffee for a future stranger. These coffee credits could then be used by anyone who may not be in a position to pay for their coffee that day. This simple act eliminated the need to ask, and reduced the feelings of shame (on both sides).

Chris Anderson, the founder of TED has recently written a book about the power of getting better at giving. He has featured the story of my friend and Suspended Coffees in his book. So my ask is that you read his book: *Infectious Generosity*. Why? So that together we get better at anticipating the ask and improve our asking and giving skills.

#50:

My first thought after reading this question was... okay... isn't the answer (for everyone): *Can you help me?* and isn't the "why" (for everyone): *Because it's too hard?* Maybe it isn't universal. Maybe it's just me! But it really feels like "the one ask" is tied to "the big problem." And the big problem feels like it's about isolation, the worst kind of independence, anti-community. Talk of vulnerability seems to be everywhere now, but maybe we aren't talking enough about the potential (terrible) side-effects of vulnerability. If I ask for help, you might say no. And if you say no, I might... feel really, really awful. I might doubt myself. I might be embarrassed. I might really suffer. So maybe the ask, turned inward, is something like: *Do you dare? Can you?*

#18:

Can you help me?

Why is it so hard for me to ask for help? Will someone laugh if I ask them to help me learn to screen print or edit video? Will they laugh at my dreams when they are starting? And if I ask for help with something more serious, like how to deal with lingering grief, will they understand what I am really asking?

When I ask "Can you help me?" it hits differently. It's about vulnerability, opening up, saying that no matter who I am in life, I still need help.

Why is it difficult? Pride, maybe. The idea that I can do it all, that I don't need help. Or embarrassment that despite being all grown up, I still don't have answers. But that's just ego talking.

The truth I wish I could remember? I am not alone in needing someone, and asking for help and getting it is like you take someone else's strength, expertise, love, and you mix it into your own life, creating something new, something powerful, and unique. It's connection and collaboration at its finest and sets you on a new path.

#71:

"Please can you explain that to me a bit more?"

When someone shares an idea, my dancing mind and my ego conspire.

My dancing mind runs off with the concept, skitter-scattering over possibilities and linked ideas, applications and uses. Excited and surface level, I want to play with things straight away, not necessarily understand them deeply first. And that's OK, that is how I learn, initially.

But then - clang. My ego shuts the open door behind me to deeper understanding.

Afraid that if I ask for more clarification, I'll look like an idiot. Slow. Stupid.

Afraid to inconvenience someone by asking them to go deeper.

And, actually, a realisation as I type: afraid not only that I'll look stupid, but that I am stupid.

I miss out on more layers of learning, my own, as I go deeper rather than just nodding and smiling, and witnessing the learning of the other person, as they go deeper too.

It's time to ask, despite - indeed because of - the fear.

#78:

"Please give me some space."

Some people are a lot of things to many people, and it can be overwhelming at times. Those people often help others before themselves, which is a beautiful thing, but not if they aren't finding the time to help themselves.

Question 8

Discount day

Let's dig deeper into the power of asking. The next time you go into a coffee chain or deli, ask for a 10% discount. If they ask why, be honest and say you thought you would give it a try.

Tell us how you felt before and after the ask.

Was it successful?

#71:

I'm not going to lie, this challenge has kept me up at night. I've felt sick just thinking about it. I bottled it twice this morning before I drummed up the courage to do it.

And now I feel UNSTOPPABLE.

And connected.

The barista was lovely. We had a chat about the weather (very British). I asked her for the discount, no fluff, straight up. She replied, "Sure, do you mind if I ask why?"

I told her I was doing a challenge, and was trying to be brave. I showed her my shaking hands, and thanked her profusely. Maybe I should have upheld the pretence, but we had a great conversation about the courage to ask. She gave me a 20% discount. I asked to pay a coffee forward. She refused, saying she would do that anyway. She gave the next guy his coffee free. We all had a chat, and we all left grinning.

This is the first question I have combed the channel answers for first before adding my own. The first I considered not doing. I'm so glad I did.

I will be paying coffees forward much, much more. We'll see about asking for the discount.

#50:

The amount of horror I felt before making the ask really can't be overstated. I struggled with finding value in the challenge, and settled on self-directed humiliation as a way to build tolerance for discomfort. And then about ten minutes before I entered the coffee shop, I read #30's post, and it confirmed everything I feared: that the exchange would make me and the server uncomfortable, that this distress would linger into the future (possibly indefinitely!), that nothing good (or just not terrible) would come from all that bravery.

And yet, I really felt I must do this weird thing. I felt resolved not in spite of #30's experience, but because of it. If #30 could sacrifice a little dignity, then so could I… (I guess?). The exchange itself was not much to write about.

The barista panicked.
I panicked.

We moved through it.

I even got the discount.

But what sticks out to me now is the cheerful feeling I had leaving the coffee shop, hard-won Americano in hand. This wasn't about the 40 cents (how much would I pay, in fact, to avoid embarrassment? I think I'm in good company when I say exponentially more than that). And it wasn't even about having successfully done something hard (for what kind of pride can you take, really, in doing something difficult you felt you HAD to do?) I think the boost came from feeling like I was a part of something, that I had continued a conversation in some embodied, potentially meaningful way.

Maybe #30's encounter alone wasn't transformative or positive… but together? In a greater context? Maybe it is essential for telling some bigger story of fear and failure and community. And isn't that sort of… incredible? That someone else's experience (far, far away) has made me feel connected today in the most joyful, big-hearted way.

#25:

Bear with my more analytical brain...

This experiment (let's be honest, it's a live human test) explores the principles of "opportunity costs."

The potential gain (P) from the discount (the benefit = B) might be outweighed by the psychological discomfort or social stigma (the cost = C) of making such an unorthodox request.

$P = B - C$

Our outcomes are either:

- A successful discount with minimal discomfort means a $P>0$;
- A denial with moderate discomfort means $P=0$; or
- A significant embarrassment with no financial gain where $P<0$.

Quantifying the cost of discomfort (C) is tricky. As someone who is more introverted, I probably have a higher C than someone more blasé and willing to brush off rejection. So the likelihood of a net-positive P (my gain) is smaller, and gets smaller the more I think about it!

So... I needed something to increase weight to that side of the equation, in anticipated fear of rejection (or even the discomfort of simply asking). My conclusion therefore, was to offer value back to the barista in the form of feedback in exchange for a % discount of their choosing. Thereby creating a negative cost for me, but one which could lead to a better customer experience for the cafe.

So the equation now becomes:

$P = B + F - C$

Where:

- B is potentially higher: The business might be more inclined to grant a discount in exchange for valuable feedback.

- F adds value: Providing constructive feedback can be seen as a positive action, contributing to a sense of fulfilment or positive engagement, thus adding value to the overall equation.
- C is more justified: The cost is not only psychological now but also involves a tangible effort that has a clear purpose, potentially making the cost more acceptable or even lower in psychological terms.

The result? I've just come out of the cafe with a free coffee (win for me), the cafe got a five star review (a win for them) and I've made a new friend at a killer coffee joint.

Who says economics isn't fun?

#85:

As a student, I lived near this small Turkish bakery. One day I came in and asked what I could buy for 3 euros (as I didn't have much money left at the end of the month) and if he could decide for me and surprise me. He sure did, as when I came home, I found lots of goodies that cost way more, including a small note that I could always come back if I needed to. I thought this was such an incredibly kind gesture.

Nowadays, I still go back to this bakery, and I have paid forward several times, as I wish others this wonderful experience as well. This week, to join the challenge, I went into a coffee store and asked them what I could do for them in return for a 10% discount on a cup of tea. I had to sing a song, so I sang my heart out, leaving the people in the shop and behind the counter with a big smile.

Meet the members of Fax Club

Why did you choose your Fax Club number?

Is there a story behind the anonymity?

#24:

I was born on the 24th and my favourite place to visit is Nepal, specifically the route from Lukla to Everest. The photo is of the runway at Lukla, it's mad that it has a 24 painted on it!

#18:

18 is the square root of 324, and we all know about 324.

#15:

I immediately thought of my favourite numbers on the back of sports team shirts. Rugby union numbers hold the greatest weight for me because they are uniform and passed on from one generation to the next. I was a fly-half during my playing days but number 10 was already taken. However, number 15 was free and reflects the number of players in a rugby team. The image I used was a vintage England rugby jersey with the number 15 on its back. I love the simplicity of vintage rugby shirts and the amateur ethos they celebrate.

#74:

Born in 19... 74. Turned 50 last year. Need to celebrate with something special.

#95:

23 was taken. So, I chose 95: simply, my house number!

My original profile pic was a mixtape. As a child of the 80's, it was in honour of the role music played in my life. '95 was the year I moved to London and quickly became baptised into the club scene and bass culture! My second profile pic was a photo I took, looking up through a skylight one day whilst visiting my son who was very unwell. I was in awe at the sunlight shining though the seagull's translucent pink webbed feet, it was beautiful! Little moments of joy matter in challenging times.

#22:

It's a master number that has huge resonance in my life.

#98:

It was the 3rd September 1998 and the first day of my first full time job after University. I was asked to send a fax from the office in the Cotswolds to the Royal Borough of Greenwich Planning Department. Hence the number 98, printed in green.

#42:

There's the obvious Douglas Adams answer. But really, last year I turned 42 and spent my time in search of the meaning of life, the universe, and everything. Fax Club was the perfect partner to my quest.

Question 9

A tale of two letters

One of the most famous experiments that uncovered the possible impact of visualisation was led by Australian psychologist Alan Richardson.

Richardson divided basketball players into three groups. The first group practised 20 minutes of free throws daily, the second group visualised themselves making free throws perfectly (but did not physically practice), and the third group did neither.

The results stunningly showed that the second group who only used visualisation showed a significant improvement in their free throw skills and were almost as accurate as the ones who physically practised. On the other hand, the third group who did nothing at all regressed in their skills.

Richardson's results show that visualisation could be a powerful tool to improve performance, and likely be even more powerful when paired with physical actions.

Now, with this in mind, imagine writing a thank you letter to the one person who has helped you the most. Imagine what you would say, how it would make you feel. Imagine posting it. Imagine the other person reading it, and how they would feel reading your words.

Now, imagine one day receiving a letter from someone you had helped, thanking you for changing their life. Imagine how you would feel reading it. Now, imagine how you had helped them.

The question this week is, how did you feel after you imagined the two letters?

#13:

FAX CLUB

RECIPIENTS: #00–#107

SENDER: #13

SUBJECT: Fax#9

MESSAGE:

Q:
How did you feel after you imagined the two letters.

A:
<u>I felt sad that I had never bothered to take the time.</u>
To tell them about the impact they have had on my life.
To let them know how much they influenced my choices.
To tell them just how much they mean to me.

Then on Tuesday serendipity struck!
I received a thank you note from someone I've been mentoring.
I felt immense gratitude that she'd taken the time.
Which brings me full circle, it's time to write a letter.

LOVE #13

#06:

As a rock climber, I know first-hand how visualisation aids performance.

This visualisation raises tension for me.

When I write my letter…

I access my child-self and it opens me to strong emotions.

I fail to adequately express the gratitude I have for this person.

For how they impacted and shaped my unfolding life.

For the energy and inspiration they ignite in me that I could not find in myself.

Bottomless thanks, that I am more, and I am better, because of them.

And foreboding sadness knowing one day we will no longer be here. Ever again.

I cry openly, almost sobbing when I write this letter.

When I receive my letter…

I have to work hard to open myself to accepting their words.

It's difficult for me to take in their letter, to own it, in the way that I want my letter to be owned.

And I know to not do so is a slur, it's disrespectful.

To not do so diminishes their act of honest vulnerability.

It's just damned rude.

#50:

I was weirdly disappointed the challenge asked me to imagine these things rather than do them. And yet… of course I shouldn't need a stranger to coax me into gratitude.

Did I write the thank you note? No.

Did I imagine it? Vaguely. Half-heartedly. On and off for disjointed, brief moments.

What did I feel? I can hardly say.

Mostly I knew how I should feel, and since I didn't sit with the challenge long enough to have my own real experience, the "should" feelings almost bored me. Lulled me. Then abandoned me.

I think the counterintuitive conclusion I came to, though, is valuable: that sometimes asking more of others gets better results. Asking for more presents an opportunity, and that opportunity might inspire or scare or humble. I'm always afraid of asking too much. And yet asking too little may leave the other person a bit insulted. Why are they asking so little when I have so much to offer?

#71:

This question holds intense poignancy for me.

The letter is for my Dad.

He will never read it. Instead, I will tuck it into his shirt pocket before the funeral, and the ashes will mix, forever a part of him. He died a week before I wrote this answer, but Parkinson's and dementia stole him away long before.

My soon-to-be letter contains multitudes. How much we loved each other. How grateful I am to carry his genes and his memories. How frequently my daughter mirrors his curious, cheeky expression as she grows. Thankfully, most I told him - before - but there are already new snippets to share. Instead of myself, I now talk to him. I look for signs, even though I don't really believe. I learned that love keeps growing after death, like hair and fingernails. And that the memories of the last years of illness have quickly peeled away like cheap paint, and the vibrant mural of his life essence is glowing again, bright and strong. I feel so bloody grateful.

And if I got a letter like this? I'd consider it a life well lived. I'll dedicate the rest of my life to loving people the way he loved me.

Question 10

Sociable media

You wake up tomorrow and you've lost all of your social media channels, yet in 12 months' time you've had your best ever year of business.

What did you do to make that happen?

#101:

What did I do to make happen?

Network more, connect with the local community and follow Cal Newport's advice to do less to achieve more.

#26:

I spent 3 hours 21 minutes a day coming alive in the real world.

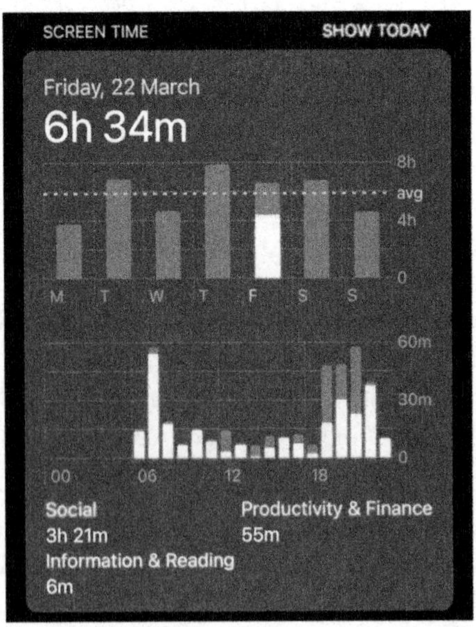

#71:

I patchily use social for three purposes at the moment:

1. To remind my network I exist and, if they happen to be experiencing a challenge when their eye falls on my profile picture, they might consider me as their solution
2. To get and stay connected, to do the above
3. (And, sadly, this is by far and away what I mostly use it for) to inspire or more likely distract myself.

My work comes from connections, no question, so if I can't use the networks to reignite those connections, how else could I do it?

- Eat aesthetic foods pointedly outside potential clients' offices?
- Ask pithy questions about work-life directly to them, possibly on their commutes, roving-microphone-style?
- Hand people newspaper clippings of articles I like? My Mum still does this to me...

I notice the above is all about broadcast. Making noise. And consumption. And yet my work, my best work, is the opposite.

So maybe my best year comes after The Year of Listening. No noise from me, just curiosity. Inviting space. Presence. Stillness. Exploring, not expounding.

And then opportunity can flood in.

#18:

Sometimes you have to disconnect to truly connect.

When you cut out the noise, you start hearing your own voice louder and clearer.

That year, without the constant buzzing of social media, it was all about getting down to the basics, focusing on the craft, the design: the real interaction with the customers.

I was able to dive deep into my work, uninterrupted, and that pure, unfiltered creativity. It resonated. People felt the authenticity, the innovation. I was making things that were for sale, not selling things that I made. I focused on the making. Rather than pushing posts, I collaborated directly with visionaries, and we created something special. Sure, maybe I did not reach every potential customer without social media, but the customers who know, know.

Rather than pushing out social media posts, I pushed boundaries.

#98:

Let's do lunch.

My socials are full of people I don't truly know. We have no stories together and no shared experiences, but I 'like' their posts about a holiday in Spain or an average looking burger. It often feels a bit soulless and far removed from the human connection that created, well, humanity.

Without social media, I'd build a fresh network of in-person friends, clients and collaborators. I founded my own business in that way. Three months of breakfasts, brunches and lunches. It was hard work and exhilarating. But, it created a strong bond, the effort was rewarded and the work rolled in.

In all honesty, those contacts have remained incredibly loyal and supported me through the highs and lows of life, with much laughter along the way.

So, when this experiment is over, lunch is on me. It might be the start of a wonderful new relationship.

Question 11

Rock around the clock

Can you spend the next 24 hours without having a single negative thought?

How far did you get?

How did you feel afterwards?

#73:

Stop the negative thoughts?

I feel we may 'need' negative thoughts. They may serve us.

So, might there be a different goal?

Perhaps stopping negative 'rumination', where negative thoughts spiral and compound, is a more realistic goal.

Perhaps a more helpful goal could be to notice and accept those thoughts, and more intentionally CHOOSE whether to engage with them.

In my experience, negative thoughts can arise from a 'part' of you (*Internal Family Systems*, Schwartz 2023). Or from 'saboteurs' (*Positive Intelligence*, Chamine 2012).

In both cases, the thoughts are framed as playing a role in 'trying to keep you safe'.

That they have your best interests at heart.

And that they might be trying to tell you something important.

So, might choosing whether to engage with the negative thoughts, or not, be a healthy reframe?

The THINK framework can provide some scaffolding here to gently question a thought:

T	Is it True?
H	Is it Helpful?
I	Is it Inspiring?
N	Is it Necessary?
K	Is it Kind?

I believe this framework can encourage one to gently query any thoughts, especially those that could be categorised as 'negative'.

To close, I find the train station analogy helpful.

The thoughts are the trains, you are the station.

Choose whether or not to board the train.

Be the station, not the train.

#03:

I lasted about five minutes! In fact, it was quite shocking how frequently the negative thoughts appeared as I don't consider myself a particularly negative person. So, noticing that was the first thing.

Started a few times, and kept thinking this is stupid, I can't do it. But the attraction of 'what could be' kept me going. It's felt like training a muscle.

So, if thinking positively, or just less negatively is like getting fit, then I'm still at the early stages of going to the gym. I shouldn't give up just because my belly hasn't shifted in one session. I need to keep dragging myself out of bed with the alarm clock. I can see there might be a moment where this becomes second nature, like a habit I don't even think about. And when that happens, a bit like getting fit, my whole outlook might have shifted imperceptibly.

Wouldn't that be something?

#13:

FAX CLUB

RECIPIENTS: #00-#107

SENDER: #13

SUBJECT: Fax#11

MESSAGE:

Q:
Can you spend the next 24 hours without having a single negative thought?

How far did you get?

How did you feel afterwards?

A:
No!
I got as far as reading this question.
I've been waiting all week in anticipation.
I was looking forward to the fax machine springing into life.
I hoped for a question that I could really delve into.
But when I received this, I was disappointed.

LOVE #13

#71:

When I completed this fax club challenge, it was three weeks after the death of my Dad, and I was in a sort of liminal grief space between death and funeral, with a major academic deadline also hanging over me. Negotiating this, while deciding how to (and if I should) show up for my clients, kept me busy and exhausted on top of the exhaustion of grief.

This question felt deeply important though, and I discovered how much unexpected joy and connection exist beyond death, alongside the heartbreak. I've always leaned into optimism, and I know I also use it as a coping mechanism - sometimes healthily, sometimes not so much. Attempting a deliberate 24 hours of positivity had me observing my thoughts more than usual, tasting each one's flavour and tone.

Here's what I learned: I can't cut off the negative thoughts before they arise, but when they do, they merit a little scrutiny, so I can understand them, and then choose what to do next.

A real example: I feel annoyed when my husband asks me to get up and get him a drink. I realise it's because I want to feel cared for, rather than the carer - but I didn't ask him, so he didn't know. I let go of the resentment, fetch him a drink, smile at his gratitude, and ask him to take care of something for me, which he does, and I'm grateful. Negative thought turned to positive action.

I learned that it isn't about eradicating the sad or forcing toxic positivity, but instead about allowing space for the juxtaposition of both. Meeting things with equanimity. Making peace with what is. And making a conscious choice as to how I react, a chance to practise compassion in all its forms, including the sometimes elusive self-compassion.

Question 12

The richest person no one knows

Today is Bitcoin halving day. It happens every four years. This is the day when the reward to the miners is halved. This halving event has a profound impact on the supply, effectively reducing it by half.

The Bitcoin white paper appeared on October 31, 2008, on a cryptography mailing list: the Genesis Block.

The first Bitcoin block and the basis of the entire Bitcoin trading system in place to this day, was mined on 3rd January 2009.

On the Genesis Block was this message:

"The Times 03/Jan/2009 Chancellor on brink of second bailout for banks."

The creator of Bitcoin was Satoshi Nakamoto. No one knows who they are. They own 1.1 million Bitcoin. That would put them in the top 20 richest people in the world.

But Satoshi has never sold one.

Bitcoin has no CEO. No marketing department. No head office. Yet, it was the fastest asset to a trillion dollars in history. Faster than Apple and Google.

So, what was Satoshi's motivation?

#18:

The question assumes there is a Satoshi. Think Keyser Söze from, "The Usual Suspects."

And if not one person, but a few, why would they never come out to take some credit?

Ever know someone who invented a multi-billion dollar idea that had such an impact, made people think about money differently, who did not want credit?

So maybe they are shy, or trying to keep quiet, or avoid the tax man. Or maybe, perhaps more likely, they helped come up with a way to facilitate payments of drugs, arms, and human trafficking since they were involved in these things. Someone like that certainly would not want the scrutiny that comes with fame.

While I have FOMO for all the crypto billionaires, I think that lack of transparency in money transfers reduces the friction in illegal activities.

So Satoshi, if you are in Fax Club, prove yourself, and transfer a million or two (or more) to #18 and each of the others.

Until then, #18 is not a fan.

#103:

I have no idea. There are two reasons for this:

I have come to realise (relatively late in life) that I am unable to fully and thoroughly understand something unless I can see, hear, or experience it. I can't see, hear or experience Bitcoin, therefore I can't really ever properly understand it. People explain it to me, but a week or two later I am in the dark again. I don't understand how something that is essentially nothing can have a value.

Why have two economies to struggle with, when one is plenty?

#25:

What if Bitcoin were less of a financial instrument and more of an artistic statement? Satoshi might be more akin to a modern-day Marcel Duchamp, placing a urinal in the gallery of global finance, than a cryptographer, asking what makes something truly valuable.

The brilliance of Bitcoin as art could be in the fact that it doesn't just sit in a gallery inviting contemplation, but infiltrates the market; testing its theory by interacting directly with economic reality.

Or, you know, it could just be a kid in their bedroom accidentally triggering panic across the global financial system simply as an idea for their science project. Either works.

#24:

Their motivation is to build a community, free from control.
Sound familiar?

#98:

Human evolution.

Research undertaken by the Natural History Museum discovered that early humans in East Africa had, by about 320,000 years ago, begun trading with distant groups, using colour pigments and complex tools. It was a medium of exchange to co-operate with one another.

Objects evolved to tokens, tokens evolved to coins, coins evolved to notes, notes evolved to cards, cards evolved to digital transactions.

Bitcoin is the next iteration of trading. Technology is the currency.

No individual should ultimately own currency. I would like to think that Satoshi understood that, instead accepting a place in history, with a basic motivation to evolve our understanding and approach to trading at a global scale.

How many bitcoins for a mid-level fax machine? I'm open to offers!

Meet the members of Fax Club

How did you get hold of your fax machine?

#48:

Not surprisingly I didn't own a fax machine at the start of this experiment but I live in a small village with an incredible community and I knew there would be someone local who could help me. I put an email out to the village and sure enough a wonderful gentleman offered to loan me his fax machine. When I collected it he told me it was one of the few things he had left from a business he previously owned and he kept it as a reminder of those happy times. I agreed I would borrow the fax machine for a year and then return it. I felt the weight of responsibility as I lugged the brown beast to the car. I sadly never did get the fax machine to work but it sat on my desk throughout the experiment whilst I received my weekly fax via an online eFax system. It became part of my office, a stable friend. Then pretty much, a year to the day, I received an email from the gentleman simply saying, "Can you return my fax machine please?" So I did.

#78:

I bought my machine from eBay. I had to order toner separately.

My very noisy fax is at my parents house. My sisters, niece and nephew saw it. They heard it every week, yet weirdly just accepted it and never really asked why! I showed my niece (aged 8) how to use it and we sent a few test pictures to some fax club members. It was all going well until we got two kittens before Christmas & they ate through the wire.

Question 13

Let them in

It's 8.30 am. You drive past a lay-by with a big lorry parked up. The back doors are open. In the cabin the driver is fast asleep. In order to keep thieves out, they let them in.

How can you use this thinking in your business or life, to help you achieve what you want by doing the opposite?

#26:

For me, open doors are similar to a mindset I have regarding health and exercise.

I don't have any rules about what I can or can't eat, or how much I move.

Instead, I can eat anything and do as little exercise or as much as I want.

You quickly realise that the open doors to junk food and no exercise are a deterrent to feeling great, and the outcome is, you don't enter.

#05:

We have a key client who always creeps the scope. We never say no, we never put our costs up. We always go the extra mile to delight them.

We are currently on our fourth iteration of the original contract, which has got bigger each year to include the things we delighted them with in the previous contract.

We have grown our income by not charging for extras.

#06:

This has me imagining that I give away everything I produce freely at no charge.

My writing, my worksheets; any and all books I write. These don't have value.

Books sit on shelves unread or never revisited. Worksheets are filled out after the fact, by rote, with little love or connection.

What has value is my presence in conversation, in relationship, in partnership.

The doors to my cab are closed when I'm resting because I'm the thing of value. The impact I create when I'm present with people is what has value. The intentional impact I create when I'm in the room with you, it's about what I unlock and open for you.

A friend once gave his book away for free for a limited period. The interest and referrals that were generated boosted subsequent sales massively.

#18:

I have limited time and time is what I sell.

But I let people pick my brain for free.

Some people think it is giving away good information. "Charge them for it!"

I see it is leaving those doors open.

I will not run out of value.

They might take something and use it, but if they want the real keys, they will come back.

Time and insight are money, but for me I think of it as if you let people see the first ten minutes of a great movie, will they really walk away satisfied?

Question 14

Tiny pieces of grit

I push the door shut. But it won't close. So this time I push a little harder, it still won't shut. This time I give it all my effort. It still won't shut. I look down at the floor, and there is a tiny piece of grit. I sweep away the grit, and gently close the door shut.

What little thing in your life or business if removed would change everything?

#71:

Honestly, my inner critic is such a drag.

Sarcastic, sneaky, determined not to let me, 'get ahead of myself'.

I know she's just there to protect me, really. I know she's only trying to help.

If she could just keep the volume down a bit, that would help. Maybe pass the mic to my inner cheerleader, every so often?

It's not so much a grit removal, more a recalibration. Sometimes I need the grit.

Just not all the time.

#18:

If there were one thing I could remove that would make a big difference in my life, it would probably be the idea that there are things that, if removed, would make a big difference. I really think that removing whatever it might be, big or small, will leave me with the next thing to focus on as self-limiting. There will always be that fly in the ointment, the grit in the hinge, the stone in the stream. You can sit on the shore and wish that stone to be gone all you want and nothing changes. But if you admire how the water simply moves around it, then you are better off. I worked on a project for this multi-billionaire who could not have been nicer. It seemed everything he touched turned to gold. So I asked a business partner of his what he thinks the secret is, and he said without pause, "He doesn't quarrel with the weather."

#11:

This question is very timely. I actually had the door and grit problem this week. It caused me to be innovative to solve it: a sturdy knife and a very thin bit of sandpaper.

I think the grit is there as it's just not enough of a problem. I'd felt the grit the last few weeks. Didn't bother to do anything about it. Only when I realised it was causing an arch scratch on the floor did I bother trying to resolve it.

So, my takeaway from this is the grit can get you to do something, and also the grit is there as we cannot be bothered to put in the effort until it becomes a big enough problem.

Is it worthwhile trying to solve grit issues? Is solving them actually the key to a much better life? Or would doing so just distract us from actually doing what we do?

#03:

I'd remove my worry about how the future will turn out.

I have an ongoing sense that I'm running out of time... and then the procrastination sets in.

If the worry wasn't there, the irony is that I think I'd not only get more done, but I'd enjoy the here and now more easily.

Question 15

Rules to live by

What key principle in life or business do you swear by that others deem to be unimportant.

What is it and why do you think they are wrong?

#98:

The Kindness Project

Kindness can be perceived as a weakness by some. An unnecessary exchange or an unforgotten component of every day human interaction.

For me, kindness is the catalyst for a wholesome, healthy and productive life.

Kindness results in a ripple effect. It has both a physical and psychological impact on our bodies. It can drive performance, create opportunities for honest conversations and build strong connections.

Kindness in leadership creates trust, improves confidence and grows talent.

Kindness in society forges community and results in a much stronger sense of belonging and value.

Create your own kindness project. It can be something simple. I leave a handwritten note saying 'thank you for doing an amazing job', for the cleaner in every hotel I stay in. It creates a sense of appreciation, it often results in a story and it always makes a difference to the individual that receives it. Try it. It will change your life and it will change your business.

Be kind, and the rest will follow.

#79:

Don't read this, it's not important.

10 rules for life and business I swear by.

1. Get to know you, and what you need. It's not selfish, it's a necessity.
2. Creativity is what will make you interesting.
3. Uncertainty, embrace it.
4. Nature, spend time with it.
5. Less but better. Focus on what you already have.
6. Kindness, it echoes.
7. Do nothing, let your mind settle.
8. Listen more than you talk. That's where the magic happens.
9. Play, have fun. Let's not take ourselves too seriously.
10. Feelings matter, they are valid.

In my experience these are not valued as much as they should be, as it's not about money or power.

#48:

To listen more than you speak.

Active listening is a completely undervalued skill in today's society. Everyone is communicating and sharing, the world is awash with information and advice but how many people are actually listening to understand? I don't mean listening to your audience so that you can deliver the solution to their pain point. I mean sitting alongside another human being and listening to their perspective. Taking in their words and acknowledging their experience. It doesn't mean you have to agree or take any action. Most people simply want to be heard, yet who is really listening?

I wonder what the world would look like if more people felt heard. I'm pretty sure it would be a brighter and more peaceful place.

Try it out, next time you see another human, actively listen to what they say and acknowledge them. Their face will light up and their troubles will seem lighter. That's a pretty special gift to give to another human and it doesn't cost anything at all.

#85:

“Not all those who wander are lost” (from J.R.R. Tolkien's poem "The Riddle of Strider”).

I love to explore new fields of work. For a long time people told me: “Focus, focus”, “Spend 10.000 hours to become a master”, “Stick to a plan”. Nowadays, connecting different words, fostering collaboration and creating bridges and bonds have become my defining strengths, where I truly thrive. The saying “When luck meets a prepared mind” resonates deeply with me. Readiness is key, but it is my flexibility and mental clarity that allow me to act when needed. More often than not, simply holding space proves more effective than desperately trying to take control.

#71:

It was terrible at first. I'd leave my most important task to the last possible moment, and it would rot me from the inside. My self-frustration grew in line with my fear that everything would end badly: a missed deadline, a missed opportunity. Failure. Catastrophe.

Weirdly, it never ended badly, apart from the bad feelings. I didn't like those feelings. But I didn't know how to stop procrastinating.

So instead, I embraced procrastination, and everything changed.

Now, as soon as something that scares me comes in, I spend five minutes rolling in it. I frame it as a question. I capture my first reactions. For proposals (one of my most procrastinated tasks), I have a creative brief template that I fill in in five minutes, standing up, with a coffee.

Then, I put the task down. Benign neglect. I do everything but it, and I am hugely productive on everything else.

I ignore it until it starts to burn, and then I do it. And I am so efficient. So focused. And I have so many ideas, because my brain has already made the connections and come up with the answers.

Hi, I'm #71, and I'm a procrastinator. It's one of my best qualities.

#06:

"It's never about the work. It's only ever relationships."

Everything that we do that is good requires teamwork. Collaboration.

There are no solo efforts.

Even solo efforts are supported by other people. Mentors, coaches, parents, friends.
Everything is teamwork.

Trust. Intimacy. Connection. Common purpose. Shared vision.

We are nothing on our own. Breakthrough transformation comes from groups.

Careers reward individual performance, from a place of scarcity. There's not enough for everyone. Education is about proving individual worth, being seen to have the correct answers to questions.

Yes, there is aptitude, potential and capability.
And to maximise these within an individual requires the contributions of others.

I am, because we are.

Ubuntu[1].

---

1 An African-origin value system that emphasises the interconnectedness of individuals with their surrounding societal and physical worlds. "Ubuntu" is sometimes translated as "I am because we are" (also "I am because you are"), or "humanity towards others".

Question 16

The currency of contentment

If you could measure your life in units of happiness instead of money, when would you have been the richest? What was it about that time?

#50:

Memory is tricky. Just as soon as I settle on a time, *'Oh, yes, wasn't it lovely to live in the woods and have so few responsibilities'* the less happy memories start to surface. *'Oh, right, there was the heartbreak. And great anxiety about the future'.*

So I wonder if the answer has to be now, because now the selective, random memory mining is making meaningful measurement so very impossible.

In this moment I am rich, very alive, very tired. Drinking instant coffee out of some misplaced kind of frugality. Hearing laughter coming from the office next door. And there's the light coming through the dirty windows in such a way. In days (hours?) I'll lose the memory of this ordinary moment and be on to the next. And that moment will be very rich, too, with its own units of happiness, grief, wonder. I don't mean to be obtuse!

Happiness math is just too hard, too limiting, in a way, because it assumes a greater continuity between selves than exists. But now! The heater has just come on. It means something to my present self. And it doesn't need to matter that the warmth won't translate to some other time, some other version of me.

#25:

Trying to think counterintuitively... or is this just intuitive still, I don't know... I guess my answer would depend on how we define "richness" when it comes to happiness.

If it's defined as the riches of happiness that come from lived experience, I'd say my teenage years were pretty fun, rewarding and all-round happy (in amongst the usual teenage drama).

If it's defined as the riches of happiness that come from connection with others, then it would be the heart-pounding don't-know-what-I'm-doing thrill of meeting and getting to know my now wife.

If it's defined as the riches of happiness that come from the (relative) freedom from worry, then it would be just after my university exams and the welcome lifting of the weight from years of study.

I do, however, believe in living in the here and now. So all things being said, I feel pretty "rich" right now...

#71:

"It was the best of times. It was the worst of times."

(Confession: not my line. Sorry, Mr Dickens).

True though.

Maybe I'm measuring it wrong. But when I think of happiness, I think of satisfaction.

Effort. Then pay off.

A few units of pain amongst the euphoria.

Something that feels worth it.

I don't like that I only recognise it after the fact, though.

So now I'm working on recognising the joy amongst the striving as it's happening.

The spice in the dish.

Truth is, I'm a millionaire every day.

#18:

Sitting on a girl's bed for the first time as a teenager, listening to The Smiths, achingly in love, wondering if she felt the same (she didn't).

The blissful years of being married and sharing so many firsts: first home, first furniture, etc, going to the movies, and dinner, or sitting around, just so in love and happy in our struggle to make it.

Being recognized in my field after having wondered if I would ever "make it" was also a different happiness.

Those are all really happy times, but the two times in my entire life where the "units of happiness" were beyond my mind's comprehension were seeing my wife standing at the end of the aisle and knowing this person is walking toward me and I get to spend the rest of my life walking together with her.

And the second was hearing the first cries of our children when they were born.

All of these were times of great hope.

I know that the wisest people know that every day is a chance to be supremely happy, grateful, and just as optimistically bursting with joy and hopefulness as you are on any of these other milestone days. I find tapping into that feeling is difficult, even though when I think about it objectively, I am unfairly lucky.

And hey, questioner, thank you for the question. Reminiscing about happy times is great.

Meet the members of Fax Club

What did being a member of Fax Club teach you?

#22:

I learnt to be more open to other people's perspectives and to remain open to opposing views.

#71:

I learned a lot about myself: what I really thought, when it didn't matter how I came across. What challenged me and what felt easy. What counterintuitive was for me. What it meant to show up. I remembered how stubborn I am. Somewhere along the last few years I had started to fear I was a dilettante, and this proved to me that I'm not, I'm determined. It made me braver, and also gave me some perspective.

#98:

I remembered how important it was to write. The absolute pleasure of being able to fill a blank page with words, ideas and stories that otherwise would have stayed inside the mind. I've also gained a community and a select group of incredible people for which I will always be connected via the shared experience that was Fax Club.

My cat also learned something, too. Cats are social animals. They understand our human routines and habits. Every Friday for the last 12 months, at approximately 17:39 GMT, the cat made its way to the Philips MAGIC 5 ECO PRIMO fax machine, as the paper noisily shuffled through the rollers. The experiment is over, but the cat still sits in its usual place, waiting. I miss that fax and I miss that anonymous social interaction.

#06:

I was part of creating a community without borders. I was part of somebody else's experiment, at the same time as running my own experiment. Leadership is about how we show up for each other, and the possibilities we hold collectively for the future.

#95:

I was filled with hope as the sense of community and mutual support grew and might be a model for wider, larger communities. Complete strangers showing the greatest care, commitment and willingness to share life experiences was heartening.

A space where there's a rule that we DON'T FOLLOW was liberating.

I kept Fax Club a secret from everyone, all my friends and family who now feel a bit put out! I need to keep more secrets I think ;)

#103:

Despite the fact I'm in my forties, I recently became aware of just how little I've valued my own opinion throughout my life. I knew that Fax Club would be a mix of people, including some successful entrepreneurs, creatives and business people. These are the types of people I'd normally assume I knew less than, so the fact that we had anonymity, with no hierarchy, felt incredibly liberating. I learnt to really trust my own voice. And I hope this is something I can retain in my life going forward.

#32:

I found it interesting to have online, anonymous communication. Writing insights on social media can feel like shouting into the void. In Fax Club it was refreshing to know people were actually reading comments and taking time to reflect

#05:

Some of the questions made me think about how lucky I am and what is really important to me.

#14:

I started to understand myself. Sometimes through my own eyes and sometimes through the eyes of other 'pirates'. Sometimes the topic we were writing about pushed me out of my comfort zone. Sometimes it challenged thoughts closer to home. Sometimes it was through the experiences of others that resonated, or gave me ideas. It's made me realise how much I leave everything to the eleventh hour. I need to hatch a plan to manage this one!

#03:

I learnt just how much worrying about what other people think and my relationship with deadlines and procrastination hold me back. Even in this very freeing environment, I worried about oversharing and I struggled to hit the weekly deadlines. The whole experiment has really highlighted those things for me, and strangely, meant I've become much more free of them as a result.

#25:

I learned that the best answers aren't always the loudest. The real magic lies in seeing the world slightly askew, and that counterintuition is often just a more interesting way of describing common sense.

#47:

Fax machines are a nightmare and contribute little in the way of aesthetically pleasing interior design.

Question 17

Comedic timing

Failure + Time = Comedy. What do you look back on now and laugh about that at the time was the end of the world?

#80:

Hindsight has proved that absolutely nothing was the end of my world: I have 100% success at surviving. And like childbirth (reputedly, I've not experienced it first-hand), one forgets the pain of traumatic events after a while.

But saying that, some things must have felt devastating in the moment. And there's plenty of material in my life to find the funny in across the spectrum of good, bad and ugly.

So I'm plumping for at least 50% of whatever hurt is now humour. And perhaps another 40% of the hurt is now, "What on earth was I even thinking?" Particularly when it comes to past partners.

The remainder, like the death of my much-beloved grandfather, is cause for celebration: we were incredibly lucky to have him for so long. Much missed, much remembered, much loved. Even after 30 years. And a man of gentle but almost consistent good humour. And when he wasn't: eight seconds of literal foot stamping and then disappearing off for half an hour to bake fairy cakes for everyone.

#101:

Being fired by a bunch of numpties and thinking it was the end of the world.

In reality, it opened up so many doors.

#98:

Last night a DJ ruined my life

I'd spent years assembling a record collection and building a reputation as a DJ. House parties became pubs, pubs became clubs and clubs became festivals.

However, the biggest moment was approaching. As a 24 year old, I was booked to DJ on New Year's Eve. A big venue, with big plans and even bigger ticket prices. I practised for weeks, my setlist was ready and my vinyl loaded into crates.

The night started well, but at about 10pm I first noticed that one of my vinyl crates was missing. This was long before the luxury of digital streaming, so I resorted to repetition and a few B-sides. I got away with it. At 11:20pm I accidentally hit the release switch on two large glitter cannons and 100 balloons fell from the ceiling. The crowd roared with excitement, but the promoter was less pleased.

Finally, the big moment. It was 11:59pm. I had a reel to reel machine linked to the PA system with a pre-recording of the Big Ben chimes. Then, the party would really begin.

10, 9, 8, 7, 6, 5, 4, 3, 2, 1 ... BOOM!

Silence. The reel to reel machine had blown the PA. No chimes, no music. Just silence. A silence that was soon replaced with booing, shouting and the occasional aerial object aimed at my head.

I didn't get away with it, I didn't get paid and I didn't DJ another NYE party ever again.

I still feel slightly guilty for the 500 revellers that never got to party like it was 1999. But I'm sure that I still gave them a night to remember.

#03:

I wrote out the answer to this, but even 22 years later, I can't commit it to 'paper' even in an anonymous forum. It's a silly drunk teenager story and if it was anyone else but me, I'd find it hilarious, but it's strange to find I just can't share it.

I think the feeling of shame has overridden what actually happened, which is interesting in itself as that is the memory that lasts. Goes to show that being nice to yourself has a longer impact than just in the moment. But I'm definitely laughing to myself now. Thanks Fax Club for the reminder that with time most failures are funny and not worth worrying about for long.

#78:

When someone you have yet to meet points out your typo... Looking back: what a fantastic way to break the ice and I can't help but laugh when I think about it.

Hi XXX,

Thank you so much for the invitation.
I would love to attend and have no dirty requirements (except for no cucumber, strange I know).
Can I just check if there is any sign up requirement or charge for attending this event?
Am I able to bring a colleague along if they are available?

Kind regards,
XXX

Their reply:

I'm so sorry, I couldn't resist it, but this has to be one of my favourite lines in an email ever...
"I would love to attend and have no dirty requirements (except for no cucumber, strange I know)."

Best typo of the year so far.

Question 18

It's your funeral

At Steve Jobs's funeral service, the guests were given a mysterious brown box on leaving. It contained a book called Autobiography of a Yogi *by Paramahansa Yogananda.*

"You should transfer your attention from failure to success, from worry to calmness, from mental wanderings to concentration, from restlessness to peace, and from peace to divine bliss within. When you attain this state of self-realization, the purpose of your life will have been gloriously fulfilled."

Choose your one book, and what is its lesson?

#98:

Write your own story

I've given this lots of thought. There are literally hundreds of books, both fiction and non-fiction that have inspired me. Some have moved me to tears, others have ignited my imagination and many more resulted in ideas for how I might live a more meaningful life.

But for me, the book I'd leave behind would be a simple blank journal.

Why? Because we all have an amazing story to tell and most of us never do, not even to those closest to us.

An estimated 117 billion people have lived on this planet. Imagine all of those best sellers, the page turners and the stories that could have shaped a generation.

Don't wait until your funeral. Buy a journal today and gift it to someone you know. Ask them to write their story. You never know, you might even be the lead character.

#71:

My stepdaughter is 18. I met her when she was 10, and my relationship with her is probably the defining moment in my life.

For four years, every two weeks I wrote an instalment of a book for her called *The Adventures of Skye*. It told the tale of her blue sausage dog and other soft toy friends, the story of our weekends together, and the adventures they had in the fortnight between. There were photos, complex installations, trips abroad. A toy would accompany me anywhere I went, and then write a corresponding entry. Friday evenings were often a tricky transition. She would race up the stairs to read the stories. I never missed a week, regardless of what was going on. There were five volumes.

When I read them back now, every word hums with my love for her and the precious family we were creating together, piece by piece.

I wonder about doing something similar for my younger daughter, who is now five. I'd like to share the magic, but I don't know if it would mean the same. The books were about showing my eldest that she was always with us, even when we were apart.

I think I'd give out a copy of those. A snapshot into what it is possible to create, from nothing. An ode of my love to her.

#03:

I wouldn't choose a book. Instead, I'd ask my guests to. I'd ask each of them to bring a book that meant something to them, they enjoyed or make them think. At the end of the service, I'd like them to find someone to give their book to. They can either swap or give one to someone and receive one from someone else: someone they know or someone they don't. They can explain why they like it or just hand it over, whatever they are most comfortable with, but I like the idea that everyone leaves with something they didn't arrive with and their life is potentially just a bit richer than before because someone else has shared something that meant something to them, a sort of "living library" if you will.

#18:

It would be The Bible, maybe with the number for a crisis hotline inside the front cover. While many people might treat it like an incidental gift from a service, I would hope at least one would keep it nearby and find comfort in its messages.

#14:

The Monk Who Sold His Ferrari by Robin Sharma

The one book that has had the most significant impact on my life and on others I've gifted it to.

There have been several times over the past decade when I've felt down, overwhelmed, and as if the world was against me. During those moments, when negativity seemed to spiral out of control, this book served as a powerful trigger to pull me back up.

But why has it helped me, and others, so profoundly?

The book taught me that true wealth doesn't lie in material possessions but in what I call 'life possessions': your health, your time, your relationships, and your family. It made me realise that the greatest riches are those that cannot be bought, but are cultivated through mindful living and meaningful connections.

Moreover, it taught me that not everything is as it seems. Life's unfolding is deeply influenced by how you perceive the events and circumstances around you. The way you interpret and respond to life's challenges can transform your experience, turning what seems like a setback into an opportunity for growth.

This book has not only lifted me out of negative states on multiple occasions but has also inspired others I've shared it with to embrace a more fulfilling and balanced approach to life.

#78:

The book I choose is *The Tortoise and the Hare*.

The lesson is that focus, perseverance and consistency can lead to success, even when faced with competition from those who may seem "faster" or "more capable". Overconfidence and carelessness can lead to failure despite having advantages.

A close second would be *The Hungry Caterpillar*, what a great story and style of book that is!

It's amazing how clearly you can remember reading some books as a child.

Question 19

Stubborn as donkeys

We had donkeys on the farm for a while, but over time, we decided they should go back to the person we bought them from. The guy arrived with his horse lorry and was trying to get the donkeys loaded. He was pulling them with all his might, and they were not budging an inch. I knew that feeling all too well. To my surprise and the donkeys, he suddenly let go of the rope. The donkeys were free. For a second, they didn't know what to do. They were confused. And then... they just walked calmly by themselves into the lorry.

What are you trying to force to happen in your business or life that counterintuitively might be helped by you letting go?

#102:

I've just started a new corporate job, I'm fairly fresh out of university and now I'm working in a team with lots of experience. Generally, I love that I get to work with, and learn from such experienced people. But at the end of the year, I'm supposed to be able to work on similar projects so I do need to learn quite fast. Already in the first month, I've been trying to prove myself, trying to impress, showing that I'm worth the extra time investment from everybody. I've been definitely more on the pushing/forcing end of that.

But I know that the motivation to impress or get good grades (external) never works for me. I do much worse. If I just focus on learning, growing, improving according to myself (internal), I mostly do better. Every now and then I fall into the trap of the wrong motivation. So I spent the second month just focusing on my strengths, what I know and asking lots of questions. So far I think this is working much better.

#73:

In the business of life, and the life of business, the uncomfortable truth is that I am forcing EVERYTHING.
Yes. Everything.

I'll unpack that a bit.

Tracing this back to source. I was raised in the UK in the 1970s and 80s. The main cultural script I grew up within, was 'stiff upper lip', where talking about things like feelings and needs, was not encouraged.

And in fact, when they were, they were often dismissed or shut down. So it was role modelled to me to internalise these things. To figure everything out for myself.

Winding back to the present day.

I find myself spending a lot of time in my head, rationally working out and intellectualising how I need to grow. And overthinking it to generate safety. "Hypervigilance" you might call it.

Rather than just letting things go, and EXPERIENCING things.

So I am now trying to lean into what's really going on. In the business of life, and the life of business.

To check in with myself, and into my body.
To sense what emotions I am experiencing, and what they are signalling to me.
To gently rewrite some of those emotional scripts.

This generates some discomfort.

But through this discomfort I grow and become more accepting of risk. And EXPERIENCE more.

Because if I spend a lot of life avoiding risk, then I realise I am actually guaranteeing a less engaged, less fulfilling, less 'lived' life than I may be capable of.

So I work on 'forcing' less, across all areas of life and work. To create a life and business with more EASE.

#32:

Trying to force my career when in reality I would like to pursue music full time. I'm scared if I take the plunge I will be broke, struggling and begin to think it wasn't the right choice.

I think about it everyday.

#03:

My husband and I are trying to have a baby. Unfortunately, it's not going well; miscarriages, an ectopic pregnancy and various surgeries have all been physically and mentally traumatic. Anyone who's unfortunately experienced similar will know the staggering knock-on effect to the rest of your life, often invisible from the outside.

To hold on to everything else, I placed totally unrealistic expectations on myself to excel at work, keep up with friends and family and have a thriving social life - all whilst endlessly chasing elusive medical advice. In short, I kept myself occupied to feel not just normal, but like other areas of life were a success, whilst we were miserably failing in one.

An exhausting, vicious circle that just made me more miserable. But I kept trying harder. Recently, I've also had some knee surgery. It proved to be a total game changer. I had to stop. There was a visible and, crucially, socially acceptable reason to.

What's this got to do with donkeys? Well, like them, the pressure suddenly went and everything became so much easier.

I'm back on my feet again, still trying to have a baby, still with work pressures and all the things that come with modern life, but I am more comfortable in my own skin. I feel I have more freedom to do what makes me feel good, rather than what I think I should be doing.

Most interestingly, I don't think I could have got there without trying really hard to go in the other direction first. Just like the donkeys, sometimes you need to test the tension to experience the real freedom of knowing the other way is OK.

Question 20

We don't talk about Fax Club

The Fax Club book that launched in 2025 became a surprise global hit.

The idea of 52 questions to look at the world in an awkward counterintuitive way struck a chord. Part of its notoriety was that no one knew the author or authors. There was no social media. No marketing. Nothing.

A request for someone to appear on Joe Rogan's podcast arrived and got turned down. Along with all the others. This only increased the myth.

Fax Club members can't talk about it. Their families don't even know they are part of it. No one knows.

The royalties suddenly became a sizeable chunk of money. Considering the unique and secretive nature of Fax Club, Fax Club decided to use it to fund like-minded founders who no one else would back and do so without revealing their identity.

Fax Club leaves the money in £20 banknotes on predetermined park benches and tells the founders to 'get there quick'. Inside the money parcel is a note with three pieces of advice signed from Fax Club.

What were the three pieces of advice?

#73:

1. Spend this on your why, not on your what.
2. Spend this on who you are becoming, not on who you are.
3. Spend this on your people (including you), not on things.

#03:

1. Work out who you'd most like to ask advice from or have a conversation with.
2. Be brave, get in touch with them and tell them a group of strangers is supporting you by funding your meeting. If you've picked an inquisitive mind, they might just be intrigued enough to say yes. And, if you're scared, it's always easier to say someone else has asked you to do something.
3. Pay for the drinks with this £20. If it's a coffee or a beer, you'll be able to stretch to a couple of pastries or a packet of crisps to sweeten the deal. Even in London. Pick your person wisely and it could be the best £20 you've ever spent. Go on, we're giving you permission to go for it.

#48:

1. You have all the answers, you just need to learn how to listen to yourself.
2. Be you always, no one benefits if you hide your gifts.
3. The journey is way more fun than the destination.

#80:

1. Be nimble: small things happen quicker.
2. Be bold: fortune favours the bold.
3. Be relentless: consistently keep going, even when it looks hopeless.

#74:

You were quick. Congrats!

Now, stay in the race as long as you can ;)

1. Dream BIG
2. Start small
3. Be c.o.n.s.i.s.t.e.n.t

Meet the members of Fax Club

What was it like being anonymous?

#74:

I'm part of it. Without people knowing who I am. No judgment.

And I can enter into the thoughts of others without pre-judgment.

Pure open-mindedness.

#50:

I loved being 50. Stripped from my job, my family, my degrees, my body. It wasn't until I was presented with the opportunity to be anonymous that I recognized how deeply I desired that experience. At this stage of life especially, when I am so heavily identified with my roles, it felt wonderful to be known for something else: an idea, or a paragraph, or even just a willingness. And when others responded positively to that untethered self? Sublime.

#25:

Liberating. No LinkedIn posturing, no pressure to be 'on brand', no fear of a half-baked idea tarnishing a reputation. Just pure thought, unfiltered and undiluted. It turns out, when nobody knows who you are, they listen to what you say. A novelty in the age of personal branding.

#71:

It didn't stop me from connecting with others. Instead, I connected with their words and ideas rather than their profile pics and their titles. It allowed me to be open with my answers in a way that has started to pave more bravery and openness in my day-to-day life.

#12:

Even though the Fax Club community didn't know my name or what I looked like, I didn't feel anonymous as I shared authentically through my answers and felt seen. However, I found myself trying to picture who the other numbers were based on their answers. It made me more aware of the subconscious associations and heuristics that lead me to make judgements in the absence of all the information. I found this fascinating as it made me more aware of my personal biases.

#102:

Anonymity made vulnerability easier. Without names or identities, I wasn't weighed down by expectations, mine or anyone else's. It also meant letting go of assumptions when reading others' answers.

At times, it felt strange: sending personal thoughts into the void, never knowing who was on the other side. Were they people I knew? Was this a bot experiment? But in the end, all you could do was trust that we had agreed to the same rules and were in it for something bigger.

#78:

I enjoyed being anonymous and I loved that we were all anonymous. I enjoyed that we got to know each other a little from our answers, yet there was nothing there that could let any unconscious bias kick in at any point. We were all equal and we all bought something different.

#03:

I took a while to warm up and I want to say that I wished I'd embraced it a little bit more, but in hindsight I shared some really personal things. In some ways, I'd love to do it all again, knowing what a supportive and creative group of people were on the other side. Is that the ultimate counterintuitive take on this: safe anonymity?!

#14:

With everyone being anonymous I felt I could write whatever I wanted and truly be myself. Something I feel in some areas of my life I don't always do and this was enlightening. No one judging my thoughts, everyone rooting for you and supporting your ideas.

I, like others, had a feeling lots of Fax Club were male, but when we met it was a fairly even split. Did the anonymity allow everyone to speak in a different tone to the norm?

#32:

I loved the idea of this. I have not heard of anything like this before and often there are many judgements, biases and assumptions present in the world today. Something anonymous really spoke to me. Also, I felt really drawn to the fact that this was a long term project and involved commitment, something I struggle with.

Question 21

Two minutes in the here and now

Out of 60 minutes, 58 minutes are spent in either the past or the future with only two minutes spent in the now.

What is the one counterintuitive thing that you can do to change this and therefore change everything in your life?

#48:

Be more dog!

I watch my dog with fascination and awe. He has such a wonderful life and approaches everything with 100% commitment. Whether eating, running, sleeping or playing he is focused on the task and enjoys himself. He is present. He knows he is the luckiest dog in the world. Oh to be that focused and to take so much joy from the most basic of things!

#11:

Change our understanding of what "now" is. When we think of the past, or even when we don't, it matters to us or drives us in the moment. Our now is directed by the past and the past is only the memory, but the memory is actually in the now.

So maybe we just 'own' that and accept maybe it's all one. Perhaps it's just an illusion of a past and now, as actually they are linked. You can only view the past with your current perspective and you are only having your 'now' experience due to your past.

#98:

The Final Destination is Unknown.

I've just spent two weeks with someone suffering from severe dementia. Witnessing their demise, their battles and moments of joy, has changed my life.

Their life has now ended, and their final words, amongst much confusion, were very clear.

"Don't focus on a destination or something others expect you to achieve. Just enjoy every simple present moment. Notice the beauty of the things around you and the privilege it is to witness them. Be more now."

Whilst cruel, perhaps dementia is the ultimate reminder for us to 'be more now'.

#71:

I think the only way for me is to connect to the physical. I may need to employ someone full time to follow me round and flick me in the centre of the forehead solidly every time my eyes stop focusing.

#18:

Hold your breath. Seriously. Once or twice a day, hold your breath. It's hard to worry about the past or the future when you are holding your breath. Then, later in the day, try to remember how each breath matters now, not the ones you took before or the ones you are going to take. Doubt me? Try it now. Just remember to breathe when you have to.

Question 22

Short-term dumb. Long-term smart.

True wealth is made from one big bet.

It will mean that you have seen something that only a few have.

This will require you to look like you are wrong to the rest of the world for a period of time.

The mindset required for this counterintuitive thinking is: 'Short-term dumb. Long-term smart.'

Can you give an example from your life or business of when you adopted this way of thinking? And what was the result?

#25:

I run a small creative agency, and last year we implemented an 'unlimited paid time off' policy after noticing team negativity surrounding taking time off. I wanted to remove the stigma and instil a culture of trust.

Outside reactions ranged from envy to disdain, with some dismissing it as part of the 'woke agenda.' And I must admit, I did fear that it could lead to a drop in output, however the opposite occurred.

Trusting our team to manage their own time led to higher productivity and motivation, and a 19% drop in sick days. Competitors are now adopting similar policies as we attract top talent with our generous package.

When people are treated with honesty and respect from the start, not as an 'earned right,' they often exceed expectations.

#48:

I am the only girl in the family and the youngest sibling with three older brothers. Although well-meaning, my wonderful brothers had such big personalities and presence that I naturally became the quieter one in the family.

Being truthful, as a child I sometimes felt overlooked. Looking back, I see the girl who was learning her craft. She was smart and perceptive, developing skills in listening, observing and understanding more than what was being said.

Roll on 40 years and you will meet a woman who has found her voice. I've become someone my family feels comfortable coming to for guidance. The calm, empathetic one who can help find a path forward.

I spent a childhood listening to spend a lifetime guiding.

#03:

I invested all my savings in a friend's business. Not because I did lots of research into his proposal, in fact I was borderline sceptical, but he'd run and sold a successful business before and I really believed in him. Plus, my dad wanted to borrow the money; I knew I'd struggle to say no and would potentially never get it back, so not having it available was the best solution. I faxed the bank (not as long ago as you might think!) to hand everything over.

In hindsight it was incredibly risky and stupid, but I had a feeling about it. A couple of years in I realised just how stupid it was when my friend called a shareholder meeting to explain they were days from shutting up shop. He also had the foresight that it was his moment to step back and bring in different skills.

Whilst I'm not advocating for this kind of 'all on black' approach to financial planning, that short term bet on my friend, including his ability to swallow his pride and recognise he needed outside help, became long term life-changing, not to mention incredibly lucky.

Over the next few years, the business did a u-turn and was sold. My initially modest savings turned into the opportunity to own my first home.

#06:

Let's talk about true wealth.

Counterintuitively, we know more money does not equate to more happiness. So if 'true wealth' is an abundance of specific resources, then we need to clarify what resources we are rich in.

While I don't have lots of money (though that itself is relative), I have accumulated a wealth of experiences, by following my heart and stomach more than my brain.

- I quit a PhD because I knew I was lonely.
- I took a sabbatical when I was lost, and found myself by joining an overland rock climbing expedition across the Silk Route.
- I left a successful tech job to take an offer overlanding through the Americas living out of my tent for a year.
- I quit the best-paid job of my life at Google and moved from NYC back to the UK to start my own business, out of a sense of duty.

I never had a plan. I've been told I was courageous, stupid and foolish. They seemed obvious choices. I don't feel I belong.

It's likely I look 'wrong' to the rest of the world.

Life is short. People want to do good. Relationships matter.

Relationships built around intimacy.

Question 23

People change people

Who counterintuitively do you need to spend more time with?

#24:

People I don't understand.

Weirdly, spending more time with them, when I'm fully present, means our differences help me to learn more about me, and more about how we see the world so differently. And it makes all our future encounters way better.

So for me to grow, and be a better version of me, then I need to be with others who aren't like me.

And we all know how we like to gravitate to those like us!

#103:

Anyone who is unwilling to make slightly uncomfortable life choices in order to play their part in slowing down climate change. Or, indeed, anyone who isn't up for discussing it. It makes my blood boil. But I need to overcome this, and accept that not everyone feels like I do about the issue. I need to really and fully understand where they come from in order to move on.

#48:

Being in the middle I find myself drawn to those at the other ends of life's journey. The very young and the elders have so much wisdom. The young remind me of what I may have neglected or forgotten whilst the older generations provide knowledge of what really matters.

#25:

As an introvert, I need to proactively spend more time with people, especially other introverts.

Although it might initially take a while to get going, as we'd probably all initially be too non-forthcoming! I think this could counter the (often) dominating loud(er) voices in the room. Silence often breeds thoughtful insights and deep thinking, and introverts so often offer well-considered opinions that lead to more meaningful and strategic discussions.

Anyone open to joining an introverts network?! Tentatively raised hands welcome.

#12:

My husband.

We live together so in theory we spend a lot of time together. But with full time jobs and three youngish children our time together has become transactional. Handover conversations about the kids, the state of the kitchen or whose turn it is to make the packed lunches.

Since having kids I think we have both changed, but we never really get the time to speak about it.

In the evenings we are exhausted.

It will be hard to 'find' time. But this fax has given me the nudge to make the time we do have more meaningful.

#80:

The me from 15 years into the future.
She's learned so much.

The 10 year old me.
She's still bold and fearless of the consequences.

Question 24

Problem hunters

This week, become a problem hunter.

Some of the best businesses have come from fixing a problem that the founder experiences in their everyday life.

If you see something and it bugs you, you must write it down for a week.

Of course, you should write it down using your non-dominant hand.

Right-handed? Left-handed? Use the opposite hand.

At the end of the week, pick the problem you most want to fix.

#12:

So as a leftie, the whole right-handed, left-handed thing helped me identify quite a few problems for lefties out there!

The main one that bugs me is that when you enter any gates controlled by tapping a card or entering a ticket: you have to tap/insert the ticket on the right. As a leftie, holding my card/ticket in my left hand, my instinct is to tap or insert my ticket on the left. The result is that the barrier next to me, not in front of me, opens and I have to make a mad dash to the next barrier before it closes. More often than not it closes with me halfway through it!

The solution: ambidextrous barriers!

Add a sensor that identifies the barrier the person tapping is standing in front of and open that barrier.

I appreciate that at busy times this could cause a few seconds delay if people are trying to tap and enter at the same time, but us lefties have been second-class citizens for too long, so the rest of the world can wait an extra few seconds to make life easier for the 10% of the leftie population out there. Bring on the leftie revolution!

#24:

Okay it's not handwritten because I'm working away and severely time-bound, but here goes...

Dear Dentist,

I wanted to share some suggestions on how the practice could improve its client experience based on my recent visit:

1. Avoid undermining your colleagues. I don't need to hear you are better than another dentist.
2. Ask clients what they want instead of assuming. Listen more and talk less. The ratio of ears to mouth is significant.
3. Don't assume clients can afford expensive treatments because they have Dr in their title. Clearly explain procedures, their necessity, and costs upfront. No one likes surprises especially if they hit the bank balance.
4. Provide realistic expectations from the start. Honesty is crucial.
5. Avoid rushing clients with short appointments. It might suit your operating model but it does not build trust. Ensure clients understand their options and associated costs. Educate before proceeding.
6. Always be truthful about expected outcomes. Avoid glossy versions that lead to disappointment.
7. Maintain humility. Not all clients aspire to a line-free forehead or other cosmetic ideals. Ego can be a dangerous thing. Watch out for it.

Let's see what happens!

#13:

FAX CLUB

RECIPIENTS: #00-#107

SENDER: #13

SUBJECT: Fax#24

MESSAGE:

Q:
If you see something that bugs you, you must write it down for a week. At the end of the week, pick the problem you most want to fix.

A:
~~My handwriting.~~
~~My kids.~~
~~My fellow passengers on the train.~~
~~My leaky trainer (when will it stop raining?).~~
~~My colleagues.~~
~~My teeth.~~
~~My...~~
Myself.

LOVE #13

#25:

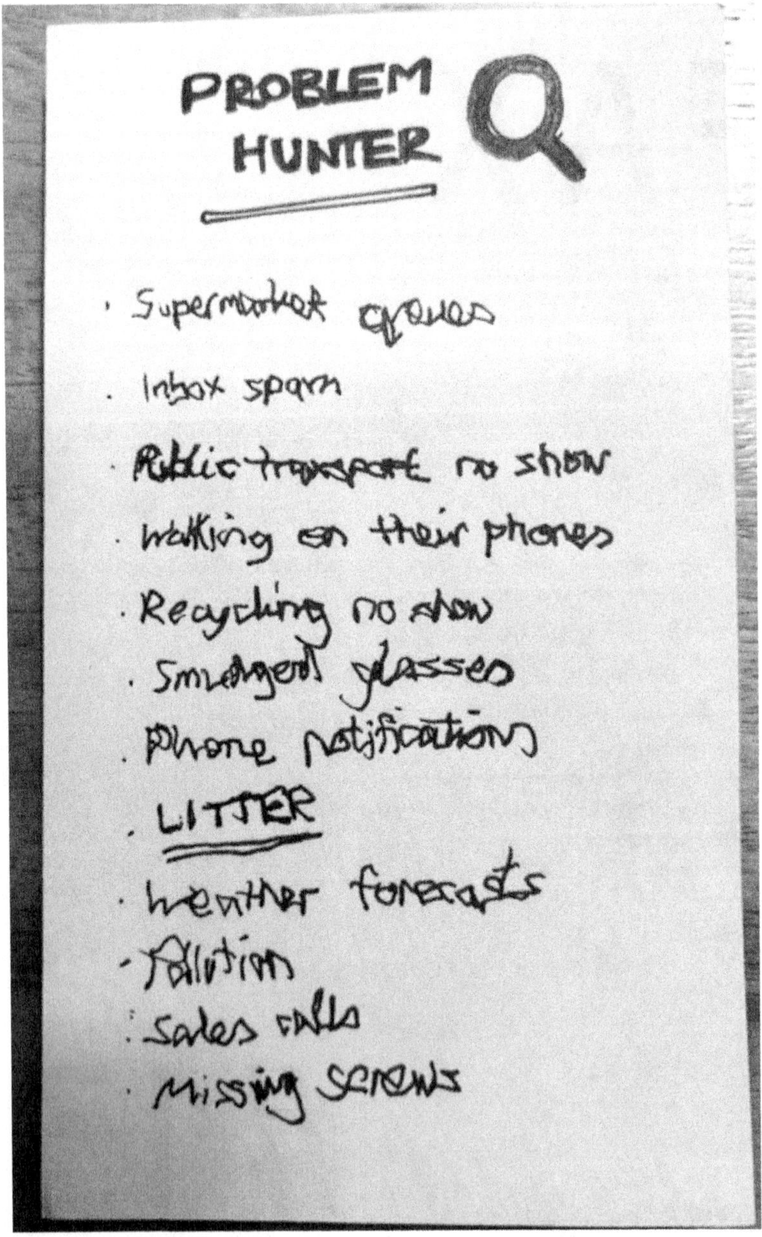
PROBLEM HUNTER
Supermarket queues
Inbox spam
Public transport no show
Walking on their phones
Recycling no show
Smudged glasses
Phone notifications
LITTER
Weather forecasts
Pollution
Sales calls
Missing screws

#18:

The rental car process.

Everything about this is horrendous.

I can go to a store and charge a sizable amount, and it takes three seconds, or go to a bank and take out the same. I can trade stocks with reckless abandon without delay. I can buy a plane ticket and board a plane much easier than I can rent a car.

However, a car rental is as though I am trying to qualify to be a pilot. And it is the same over and over. Prepay or not prepay, roulette in whether the car you were promised is the one you get, and choose the options (insurance, GPS, etc.). Make a reservation and don't pick it up, we charge you.

Sometimes.

Sometimes it is just a reservation.

Oh, and ID. Type it in when making the reservation, show it again when you pick it up. Give the same credit information.

Why is this process still so miserable?

If I join the Chairman's club you will meet me at the gate, walk me to my waiting car, and off I go.

So you are capable of excellent service, why not democratize it?

Meet the members of Fax Club

What kept you here if you wobbled?

#74:

The fear of getting ejected.

After three weeks with no answer, the group could vote for ejection. Horrible!

And more positively: the pleasure to achieve a wild challenge: writing every week for 52 weeks in the raw. Ultra-marathon for creatives.

#47:

Firstly, sheer pig-headedness. I'd made a commitment and I intended to stand by it. I knew people would drop by the wayside and I refused to be one of them. One's mother did not instil a spirit of surrender! Secondly, the people and the answers they gave. The insight into the minds of others was fascinating.

#71:

I was kind to myself. I completed all 52 weeks, even though I finished the day before we met in London! Sometimes I carried questions around with me for weeks, but I always believed I would answer all the questions. I wanted to be proud of that achievement.

#32:

I made a promise to myself to stick with it. I reminded myself of progress over perfection. Sometimes it was overwhelming to read and long answers were intimidating. However, sometimes one or two words can be just as powerful, and even have more meaning in some cases.

#48:

I wobbled many a time but I always came back. I had a note on my desk that said: "Fax Club. Show up. Remember how much you wanted this." It was a reminder to stay tuned to my why. It was never about the end goal. It was always about how quickly I could get up and try again. It was about learning from others and being part of something bigger than me.

#50:

I lost faith in the concept of a book, and at times I lost faith in the process altogether. But I never lost faith in #71. Every answer she wrote was the expression of something I felt, but more beautifully articulated than I could ever manage. And we couldn't deny that we had a sort of... weird connection. So when I faltered, I thought of #71 - my twin far away - and knew she had an expectation of my participation. It mattered to me that she finished, that I finished, and that we finished together.

#24:

Commitment. I signed up, I don't quit. I was part of something new and exciting and way bigger than me.

#38:

The inspiration I got from reading the questions, and other answers. Stubbornness. Freedom of expression.

#102:

The answers of others. Some weeks, writing, let alone posting, felt nearly impossible. But I kept coming back, drawn by the thoughts and perspectives shared. Reading them sparked something in me, a reminder of why I started. And on many days, it gave me just the boost I needed to keep going.

Question 25

A letter to the boss

It's time to put your non-obvious way of thinking out into the real world. Write an email to a CEO, founder, owner with nine counterintuitive ideas to get their business back on track.

In the email, tell them you are sending it as a fan that just wants to see their company fly once more.

Share with everyone your list of nine ideas. And tell us why you picked that company.

If you get a reply, please share it.

#78:

Dear Founder,

I WANT YOU TO SUCCEED SO HERE ARE NINE IDEAS FOR YOU:

1. Share more on social media about where you swim: locations, people you meet, things you see!
2. Share more on social media about "why" you swim: what does it do for you?
3. Tell more of your story: how did you get here?
4. Hide a product somewhere and post clues of how to find it!
5. Give your product to someone who can't swim and take them with you for a dip!
6. Wear your product everywhere you go for one week. Have fun, take photos, talk to people about it.
7. Have fun experimenting with your social media posts!
8. Make up a song about your product and perform it to your friends!
9. Give away the profit from your next sale... only you know who/where to!

FEEL FREE TO IGNORE ME ❤

Their reply:

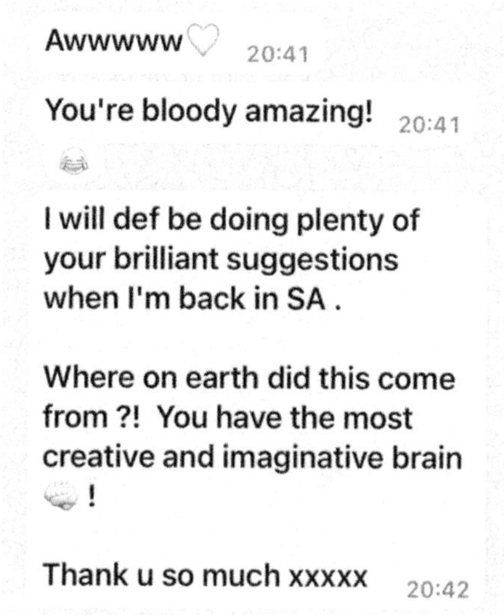
Awwwww♡ 20:41

You're bloody amazing! 😂 20:41

I will def be doing plenty of your brilliant suggestions when I'm back in SA .

Where on earth did this come from ?! You have the most creative and imaginative brain 🧠 !

Thank u so much xxxxx 20:42

#25:

My letter is to the founder/owner I know most intimately: me. I'm also the person I feel most qualified to critique. So here are some of the many thoughts that have been swirling around in my head for a while, written down in a letter to me.

Subject line: Rekindling our spark

Dear Me,
So… this feels strange, but here's something a little different: an email to you, or should I say, to me? To us? I prefer the collective.

Remember when we first started? The passion. The excitement. Back when "work hard, play hard" wasn't just a cliché, but a way of working, of life.

Our office was more than a workplace. It was a hub of creativity, camaraderie, and the relentless pursuit of brilliance.

But that was then.

The industry has shifted, and so have we.

We're navigating a labyrinth comprised of data points, algorithms and "digital-first" strategies.

The fun, the spontaneity seems to have faded.

And, let's be honest, it's taken its toll. The spark feels like it's flickering, but here's the thing: we're still here.

We're still capable of magic; we just need to fall back in love with the business we built in the first place.

So, let's start by celebrating our mistakes, rather than drowning in them. Instead of hiding our blunders, let's show them off. Learning from them can be our inspiration, our success.

It shows we're not afraid to take risks. And risks are who we are.

Imagine seeing our computers, not as machines swallowing our creativity, but as co-creators.

Let's invite them to be part of the process, not just the end result.

Data, oh data.

Yes, it's crucial, but let's remember it's the story that moves people. Not the endless numbers on the page.

Shifting our focus back to the narrative can touch hearts, not just minds.

It's what can transform mundane moments into magical ones. Every interaction, from a thank you note to a meeting invite, can be an extraordinary one.

Creativity doesn't have to be confined to campaigns. It can be in the everyday details.

In a digital age, we must remember to engage its antithesis: the world of analogue. Let's bring back Don Draper-inspired physical mock-ups, they're so refreshing and make a lasting impression.

Every interaction should spark joy.

Thanks Marie Kondo.

Let's design experiences that aren't just functional, but are delightful.

This must resonate in our culture, too. Let's set aside time for creative "play". It might sound frivolous, but it's often in those moments that genius emerges.

We've always prioritised people over profits, let's double down on that. Building deep, meaningful relationships. When people feel valued, we all profit.

I'm writing this to remind us we're not just "another creative agency", but a group of passionate people, who believe in the power to change the world. Let's re-ignite the spark.

Much love, always,
Me / You / Us

#06:

I chose the company because they have a relatively new CEO, and it's a company whose health and fitness services I have used for many years. They supported me in creating some of my greatest identity-defining achievements. They have millions of users of their tech stack.

I have not yet received an answer.

Nine counterintuitive ideas on leadership

On Goals:

- A GOAL is not a place to get TO, but a place to come FROM.
- The goal is never the goal (that's a LAG measure). It's only a vehicle for a way of being today (a LEAD measure).

On Balance:

- Work/life balance is a MYTH. Balance is the by-product of the choices you make in this moment.
- Balance reflects the boundaries you keep.

On Coaching:

- The best coaches working today work for free (sheep, cows, llamas.). Sheep tell you 'Yeahhhh', Cows tell you, 'Nooooo', Llamas let you keep talking and just stare. Which coach is right for you today?

On Leadership:

- Don't ask people their opinions unless you're really prepared to hear what you don't want to hear.
- Your most strategic work looks like your laziest (feet up, staring at the ceiling, quietly thinking about the future). Look lazy more!
- Stop doing what you're good at, and start doing what you're paid for.
- You are part of your problem. You are complicit in creating and maintaining the unhealthy patterns that play out around you.

#13:

Dear Sir,

I'm sending this fax as your #1 fan.

I'm currently a member, and it's great. I'm learning a lot about myself and others.

Having followed you for some time, it's obvious that the business is in good shape and on track. But have you ever stopped to think if it's on the right track?

You're clearly an ethical man, and I admire your passion for sustainability and community, as well as your mission to inspire people to make positive changes in their lives. In your professional sphere, you're a creative rockstar.

But is this enough?

I would wager that most of your community are older and/or more affluent, making it more exclusive than it maybe should be. Do you not think it would pay off in the long term to use your influencer status to do even more good?

What about the youth? The neurodiverse? The ones who don't fit in? The rejects?

Isn't it time to unlock their potential? Show them what's possible? Show them what they could become? They are the future after all.

Here are nine ideas you might want to think about:

1. Be more inclusive.
2. Champion the rejects.
3. Make it accessible.
4. Do some stuff for free.
5. Build them a community.
6. A home where they feel valued.
7. Create them a springboard.
8. From which they can fly.
9. And bring positive changes to their lives.

I would have written this letter by hand, but I'm dyslexic and find it hard to write. Plus, my spelling is awful.

Question 26

Five years of happy

The year is 2029. You are looking back on the last five years of your life, which have been the most happy you have ever been. A big part of your success has been down to your seven part framework for living your life. Please share it.

#03:

1. Accept that what will be will be.
2. Spend as much effort into choosing where to put your effort as you do on the effort itself.
3. Spend quality time with your parents.
4. Prioritise spending time with your siblings, niece and the friends who feel like family, the ones you can truly relax with.
5. Keep fit, and plan in realistic ways to do it that fit with what's going on at the time. Little and often is better than a big plan that doesn't happen.
6. Keep learning, starting with the language you're currently studying. It opens up not just better relationships with existing family, but another culture and a new way of thinking about communication.
7. Read as much as you can. Always have a book on the go so that dead time is filled with reading not scrolling.

#12:

What I find interesting about rowing… is that it is always done backwards. "It's almost as if the sport itself is trying to teach us not to get ahead of ourselves", from the character Dr Mason in *Lessons in Chemistry* by Bonnie Garmus.

When you row you face backwards. You can't see what is coming, only where you are and where you have been. This is an interesting metaphor for life because really we are all speeding through life backwards: only being able to see what is and what has been.

So in 2024 I developed A Rower's Framework for Life. Five years on I am the happiest I have ever been.

A Rower's Framework for Life:

1. **Have a coxswain**. In rowing the coxswain is the only person facing forward. They are steering the boat and coordinating the power and rhythm of the rowers. The coxswain sets the conditions to get the intended result. No one can see into their future, but taking the time to develop a clear understanding of what it is you would like to achieve in the next five years and creating the best conditions to get you there is like having a coxswain sitting at the stern setting your rhythm and steering your boat.
2. **Create a rhythm & flow**. When a rowing team is at its best they have a rhythm and flow that results in them gliding through the water. Find daily routines and rituals that help you to find your rhythm and moments of flow, small actions that support you in gliding towards your goals.
3. **Build endurance, strength and commitment**. Rowing is hard. Life is hard. Both take endurance, strength and commitment. Train your body physically. Train your mind mentally. Exercise. Get curious, get uncomfortable.
4. **Focus on horizontal movement**. In rowing it's the horizontal movement of the oars that get you to where you want to go. If you dip the oar too deep you expend energy for little forward movement. In life it is important to go deep at times, but forever going deep without any horizontal movement means that you are unlikely to get where you want to go.
5. **Expect a flip**. A flip is when a rowing team is unexpectedly flipped out of the boat. This also happens in life. We think we have hit our rhythm and are on our way to achieving our goals, only to find our plans or expectations flipped. Get back in the boat, learn from the flip, and get comfortable with the possibility of more flips in the future.

6. **Relax**. The best athletes make their sport look effortless. Elite rowers don't grip the oar too tightly; they focus their effort on the muscles and movements that propel the boat forward. In life only expend energy on things that get you to where you want to be. Let go of sunk costs of shame, of negative beliefs and don't grip too tightly to any dream or plan. Remember, there may be a flip on the horizon. Relax and enjoy the journey.
7. **Be part of a team**. Rowing is best done as a team. The same can be said for life. Surround yourself with people who inspire you, who will push you, who are pulling in the same direction. When you work together you will cross the finish line.

#74:

Seven part framework to live a successful life
(First try. I guess this list will evolve over time…)

1. Consider what success means for you (what are your top three answers?)
2. Spend 50% of your time cherishing the #1 item of your answer to the previous question
3. Then work to fuel (with energy and money) what you want to offer to your #1 item
4. Spend time for yourself: reading, exercising, developing your spiritual life
5. Be clear on where you want to be at the end of the year / quarter / month / week
6. Do one thing at a time
7. Get ready to change your plan when sh*t happens

#06:

See. Run. Love.

My seven part framework is embodied in this three word expression of my core values.

Seek opportunities, big and small. Act with full permission (self-authority & self-compassion). Be kind, to yourself and others. Everyone needs your love.

This is the framework that comes to me today:

1. **Life is short**: be intentional in what you choose, and the impact you create.
2. **Relationship is all there is**: every worthwhile undertaking requires teamwork. Even the solo efforts are enabled by others. You succeed because of others (Ubuntu).
3. **Say yes to new things**: experience more. Expand your range. A growth mindset fuels innovation and creativity.
4. **Be wrong more**: you are not as smart as you think. Your advice is never as good as you think it is. If you've never learned from failure you're still a rookie.
5. **Appreciate the small stuff**: the best outcome is that we all die in the right order with minimal pain (see #1). Practice gratitude and generosity. When bad things happen you still have something to appreciate.
6. **Break the damn bottle**: create from possibility, not from the lessons we chose to learn from our past. See the old Zen Koan about the "Goose in a Bottle".
7. **Move your body**: your body is incredible. Use it. Share it. Run. Climb. Dance. Love.

And there's everything else, more poetically written by others:

- "Everybody's Free To Wear Sunscreen", Baz Luhrmann
- "Nine Life Lessons", Tim Minchin

Question 27

The reverse bucket list

All kudos to Arthur C. Brooks for this thinking.

We all have a bucket list.
Let's review it with a non-obvious mindset.

Here's the thinking: You can increase happiness temporarily by wanting more. Or permanently by wanting less.

So now, go through your bucket list and keep your goals, but take away your attachment to the outcome.

You remove the attachment to the result. Your focus goes to enjoying the journey. Intention without attachment.

Every time you think of your bucket list, you no longer think of the result, but the fun of getting there.

Please share your 3-year bucket list. And the fun its pursuit could bring you.

#20:

I honestly didn't have a bucket list. But now I do...

1. **Puffin watching on Skomer Island**
   The boat ride. The anticipation of seeing these delightful birds. What other wildlife might we see? Oh I hope we see dolphins! It would mean at least a weekend away from home, so an opportunity for a mini holiday.
2. **Family holiday in the Isles of Scilly**
   The journey there by boat or by helicopter or plane. I've never been in a helicopter. How terrifying and exciting! That would stretch my comfort zone! Choosing which island to stay on.

3. **Separate 1:1 weekend trips with my son and my daughter**
   What would they enjoy? How do I want them to remember me from this time? Planning it together with them. Do I let them plan it?! Would that create more excitement for them? Maybe it could be an exercise in budget management for them. They would need to consider my needs as well as their desires, so a lesson in compromise. But ultimately a chance to make lasting memories for both of us.
4. **1:1 weekend trip with my husband**
   Can we remember who we were before life and kids took over? The first time we leave our teenagers home alone, a lesson in trust with the added benefit of boosting their confidence. A reunion family meal on our return.
5. **Get a new job**
   Gather my portfolio and find forgotten work. Remember the talent I'd forgotten I have and boost my confidence. Plus it might inspire me to make new work. Rewriting my CV and really focusing on what my unique skills are, will boost my self esteem.
6. **See the Northern Lights**
   Where will this be? Norway perhaps. And how will we get there? I could plan a road trip and visit other places en route. It would be great to include some other experiences on the trip. Embrace the snowy landscape. Ride a dog-sled. Whale watching!
7. **Build a wildlife pond**
   Sharing the process with my family and the satisfaction for all of us that we have built something worthwhile together.
8. **Make a playlist of my favourite music of all time**
   Remembering times I associate with the music while making it.

#42:

Make my business a 'business'. At the moment I feel like I'm playing. It's a moment of transformation in my life as I work out how to do this after being an employee until now. Consistency and discipline will get me there. I know what I'm doing and what I want to do. I 'just' (FFS) need to do it.

Take the family on a sailing trip. I've already said, 'If not now then when?' on this. I'm working through the qualifications and should be a Day Skipper in a couple of weeks. Then I think Yachtmaster will follow. I want to be on the water as much as possible. I love what it does to my spirit. And I love the technical challenge – I can't just be 'by' the water. I need something to DO.

Give the talk, answer the call, be the answer. This one's a bit ethereal. And definitely more about the journey than the destination. I'm looking for signs that I'm getting somewhere. Getting on stage. Having people seek my services. Being the answer to the question. This one's probably very psychologically revealing.

#88:

1. Dance more. The feeling of being in the moment and feeling: that's the bucket.
2. More people say I made them feel seen and understood.
3. Travel more. It's not about the destination but all the little moments in between that make it magical.

Question 28

Small talk, big truths

There is a truth. And always another truth that lies behind it. How are you? How are you, really? This week, make a conscious effort to ask the second question that seeks the deeper truth. Show genuine interest and be present. Notice how it changes the depth of your conversations and strengthens your connections. Share your experiences, if you are willing. How did it change the conversation? How did it make you feel?

#14:

Is it just me or does it feel like asking the question "how are you?" has recently become more of a small talk throw-away question? A courteous polite question we all ask, but how much do we genuinely listen to the answer?

How much do we genuinely 'want' to listen, especially depending on who we're asking?

Are you asking a stranger or someone you know? Are you asking someone who's always negative and drains you, or someone who's upbeat, positive and uplifts you?

How genuine is your questioning?

Can we ask "how are you?" with a tone of voice that makes people feel like you genuinely want to listen?

If someone asked you the question "how are you?", how would you reply?

"You're good, that's great. Are you really?"

I used to answer "good", but I'm now pausing before I answer.

Stop answering with your auto-reply and take a moment of pause to genuinely think about how you feel.

The more truthful and open you are, the more others seem to feel they can do the same.

I realised asking a secondary qualifier can work well to make people realise you're genuinely asking how they feel: "How are you? You look [happy/sad/tired/busy/upbeat] today."

This shows someone you've noticed how they seem today and that you're genuinely interested. They won't be used to that! They may be slightly wary of your questioning. Or relieved to be able to open up. Someone's finally asked genuinely how they feel.

Next time when you go to ask "how are you?", think...

How can I make this person genuinely feel heard?
Everyone has an innate need to feel heard.

And if anyone asks you how you are...

Pause before you answer.
Think before you speak.
Be as open and honest as you can be.

#38:

We often ask "how are you?" and sometimes get the answer "fine, thanks" and we often accept this and move on. What if instead of accepting what if we follow up with "what's the story that you wish to share with me right now"?

There's digging a little deeper.

For the last few months we have had a family bedtime check in ritual to ask three questions:

1. What was the best part of your day?
2. What was the worst part of your day?
3. What do you want me to know?

The most surprising outcome has been a greater sense of connection and ease going into bedtime and more relaxed final words. My hugs from the kids as we have had a change to listen and see as well as be seen.

Is this a basic human need?

#98:

I often get lunch from the same café. I exchange pleasantries with the owner, and then leave to enjoy their tasty sandwich creations. I don't know anything about them really, but then I have never really asked.

Today I asked how they were. The initial response was short and positive. But then I dug a little deeper and asked how are you really? Their body language changed immediately and the conversation began to flow. The owner was worried about reduced footfall during the summer holidays and their need to work excessive hours with most of their small team away. I listened and asked some more open questions. They looked increasingly at ease and I saw both their enthusiasm and fear. They asked about my business and I was equally honest and transparent. I felt a connection, a part of that person's life and I knew our transactional relationship had already tipped towards friendship. I was thanked for caring. It felt good.

From now on I will earn my lunch through honest conversation and I'll enjoy it all the more.

Meet the members of Fax Club

What was it like to finally meet in person?

#95:

The feeling of meeting family you haven't seen for decades! To feel part of something much bigger felt good, and nourishing.

I didn't want to leave, next time make it a weekend.

#22:

Amazing. The energy in the room was incredible. An incredible bunch of kind, supportive, talented people.

#06:

Meeting in person was a highlight of the project, and a big highlight of my year. Imagine walking into a room full of strangers that aren't strangers at all. You know so many deeply personal stories, just not whose stories they are!

#78:

That day was a bit surreal. On the way I was wondering if there would be two or three people only, it was so unknown! To walk into a room full of people was overwhelming, but pretty amazing too, we had plenty to talk about, plenty to connect on & plenty to do. I really liked everyone, but I couldn't help but think: "Am I good enough to be here?", "What can I bring?".

#38:

It was such a safe environment.

#14:

I was only slightly nervous, compared to a regular meeting of strangers. The anonymity felt like a leveller, everyone was in the same boat and everyone was supportive and potentially a bit nervous too!

I was excited to find out who the people were behind the numbers and pictures. What did they do for a living? Where did they live? What would they be like when you talked to them?

The energy in the room slowly built throughout the day. Everyone there was inspiring, and inspired to make 'something' happen.

#24:

I bloody loved it! The faces behind the words. I felt such affinity to some numbers, it was awesome to meet them.

Question 29

Blow the budget

You have been given a budget of £20,000 to spend on personal development. You have seven days to choose how to spend it or you lose it. It can be a mastermind, a course, or anything you choose. It has to be spent on one thing only. What would you choose? How did you find it? And what convinced you? Lastly, what was the one reason that was holding you back from picking it?

#79:

This is such a brilliant question. At first, I felt overwhelmed by it, but after thinking for a while, it became crystal clear.

I'd spend the £20,000 on a three-month artist-in-residence at a screen printing studio. (If I had more money, I'd stretch it to six months, maybe even a year.)

I'd learn to screen print (I know the studio, which helps), and I'd focus only on creating art, not worrying about earning money, winning new clients, or securing financial stability for my family.

I'd let my mind be open.

Play. Have fun. Experiment. Explore.
Get messy. Be in the moment.
Not worry about anything other than making art.

How I'd use the money.

1. Part of it buying my time so I could concentrate on the art, learning a new skill, and just doing.
2. I'd need to pay for ink, paper, desk space, and lessons from the technicians and other artists.
3. At the end I'd have an exhibition.

For years, I've wanted to pursue my art, but it's never been the right time.

The sad truth is:
Two years ago, I had the money but no time.
Now, I have the time but no money or financial security.

I've always had big responsibilities for others and never want to let anyone down.

Maybe this is a lesson from the universe.
A reminder that there's no such thing as the right time.
This is now a dream. How do I make it happen?

#32:

I'd spend it on signing up for a uni course or a music course I've been wanting to do for a while. The music course is around £1,000.

This question is difficult to answer because £19,000 would be lost in the ether. However, I need to learn to let things go and this would be good practice. In reality, I am not sure if this would actually happen however it's a good practice of focusing on what I truly desire.

The ability to say "no" and concentrate on what really matters.

The money would buy opportunities in the form of connection and collaboration with other musicians. This is the most essential aspect of studying at uni or an in-person course. It allows you to forge connections that may be a lot more difficult to find outside of that bubble. I don't need to spend more than the entry fee. It's not often I find myself thinking about how to spend more money!

#25:

I think we (or, should I say, I) often think of personal development as a solitary pursuit. One involving courses, books, and introspective exercises.

But true growth, the kind that really transforms, often happens in the company of others.

Not just from study, but in the places where we can have unpredictable and sometimes messy exchanges with people who see the world differently. It's in these moments, around a table, where real insights emerge.

So, with a £20,000 budget, I'd set up a recurring series of dinners with strangers.

The "Change Encounters Relational Network" (CERN 2.0).

These wouldn't be ordinary gatherings. Each dinner would be a carefully curated mix of individuals from different walks of life, brought together to share stories, perspectives, and, most importantly, their unique wisdom.

Their value lies not just in the conversations themselves but in the unexpected connections and the lessons that can only be learned when we step outside our own echo chambers.

These dinners would tap into the innate human need for connection, combined with the power of diverse perspectives, and serve as a catalyst for personal growth, with each interaction challenging your assumptions and expanding your understanding.

There's hesitation in this as it's a risk to invest in something so intangible, where the returns aren't immediately measurable. But perhaps that's exactly where the most significant growth happens?

In the things we can't control.

#06:

In 2018 I walked away from (what was) the best company to work for.

Since then I've invested over $30,000 of my own money in personal and professional development.

I've attended more development programs in the last few years than in 25+ years employment in the tech sector.

So I'm good right now. Thanks.

But I'm not really.
I'm sad.

'Last Chance Tourism' is a thing now. A whole industry emerging from climate change.

So here's how I expand next.

Gorillas.

I visit the mountain Gorillas and sit with them. Before we remove them forever from our blue and green planet.

I sit with them. Look into their eyes. Be present with them. Majesty. To sit with such grace and intelligence, without common language. Connected. Curious. Trusting. Present.

So different, and distant.
So alike, and interdependent.

This moves me beyond words and changes my outlook forever.
My greatest personal development.

Question 30

The book that will change your life

The book that will change your life is the one you write. What is your book title?

#101:

The Optimist's Guide to Climate Action: How We Can Win

#79:

I Don't Have the Answers. But I'll Keep Asking the Questions

#88:

You're Not Good Enough. And Other Lies We Tell Ourselves

#22:

It's an Inside Job: Everything You're Looking for Isn't out There

#98:

The Confident Introvert, author unknown

#13:

Neurodiversity: Making the Most of What Makes You Different

#49:

Our Year in the Club We Didn't Talk About

#48:

The Little Guru: The Big Lessons Children Can Teach Us About Life

#38:

Sh!t Happens! A Guide to Living a Life Less Seriously

#32:

No Recognition or Acknowledgement and Doing It Anyway!

#102:

Both/And: The Nuances of Paradoxes

#26:

Not Yet Dead

#24:

A Life of Learning

#89:

Sardines Thrown into the Sea

Question 31

Order some magnitude

You can suddenly charge 10 times what you were previously charging for your work. What one thing did you change?

#73:

I'd actually implement the advice that a recent client gave me, which speaks directly to this.

My fee for the initial piece of work was £4,000. This then led to an ongoing role for more than two years.

Reflecting on our work together several months after this, they said to me: "... in 25 years, you're the only person we've EVER been comfortable paying money to without knowing where it is going. Your entry level fee with clients should be £25,000. You should sell the journey, not the destination. Transformation doesn't overplay it."

I'd also stipulate that my clients 10x the time and attention that they think they will need to dedicate to the work, and create a commitment of challenge and attention from them.

A contract to go to the depths required.

Together.

#05:

We have almost this situation already. We can charge some clients a lot more because they want outcomes, which we know we can deliver. Other clients will only pay for activities, and they usually have their own low valuation for these activities.

So, the one thing I need to change to charge 10x more is...

We should be marketing our service based on the outcomes we can deliver to clients who really need and value those outcomes.
OK, let's go!

#74:

One thing?

Me! By that I mean, the image that I have of 'me'. The perception of my own value.

Me... diocre? Too often.
Me... dium? Not the right size!
Me... aningful. I hope so.
Me... and my ability to speak about 'me' = 'the value I bring to the world.'

I often use this expression as a 'metaphor'. I realise it is not a metaphor, it's a reality. Each one of us is bringing value to the world. Each of us is able to change the world... around him, around her.

For the value we offer, yes, we can charge 10 times the amount!

#50:

I've struggled with this one because in my field this would be... insane. So, I tried to bend it a bit: maybe instead of my service, it's 10x for my time?

And I could... do something slightly different? But even that felt nuts. Un-doable. Because "slightly" wouldn't be enough to justify that kind of fee raise.

So I've been thinking and thinking… trying to find a way to make the question work for me.

In the end: that's the problem. I'm really glued to the logistics, to the present, to the obstacles.

So the thing that would need to happen so that I could charge 10 times more… first up: a bigger imagination.

I'd need to be able to sit for some length of time in the possibility. And for that I'd need to create time in my schedule for creative visualization.

And for that to happen I'd need to value money less (i.e., work less). Though if I accomplished this feat it's hard to say why I'd be using my imagination to think of ways to get more money?

Is this… a terrible circular puzzle?

Or maybe it's the counterintuitive answer, as the conclusion is something like this: to make more money I'd need to care even less than I do now about making more money.

Question 32

A good job, according to Breslin

On November 22nd 1963, President Kennedy was assassinated. Three days later he was due to be buried in Arlington National Cemetery, it would be the biggest gathering of international dignitaries in America's history. There were 220 representatives from 92 countries: presidents and prime ministers, princes and princesses, kings and queens and emperors all coming to pay their respects. Every reporter and journalist would be writing about it, trying to fit all the grandeur in. But one reporter didn't do that, in fact he didn't report on the funeral at all, he decided that wasn't the story. He thought "What can I do that's the opposite of what everyone else is doing?"

Jimmy Breslin went to Arlington Cemetery to look for the man who'd be digging the grave, and he interviewed him. His column started like this:

> Clifton Pollard was pretty sure he was going to be working on Sunday, so when he woke up at 9am in his three-room apartment on Corcoran Street, he put on khaki overalls before going into the kitchen for breakfast. His wife, Hettie, made bacon and eggs for him. Pollard was in the middle of eating them when he received the phone call he had been expecting. It was from Mazo Kawalchik, who is the foreman of the gravediggers at Arlington National Cemetery, which is where Pollard works for a living. "Polly, could you please be here by 11 o'clock this morning?" Kawalchik asked. "I guess you know what it's for." Pollard did. He hung up the phone, finished breakfast, and left his apartment so he could spend Sunday digging a grave for John Fitzgerald Kennedy.

Later in the piece, Breslin continues:

> He is an equipment operator, grade 10, which means he gets $3.01 an hour. One of the last to serve John Fitzgerald Kennedy, who was the 35th president of this country, was a working man who earns $3.01 an hour and said it was an honor to dig the grave.

Later still, Breslin finishes like this:

> Clifton Pollard wasn't at the funeral. He said he tried to go over to see the grave. "But it was so crowded a soldier told me I couldn't get through. So I just stayed here and worked, sir. But I'll get over there later a little bit. Just sort of look around and see how it is, you know. Like I told you, it's an honor.

This piece changed the way writing is taught, it's now called 'The Gravedigger Theory' on journalism courses at university.

Breslin started out as a sports journalist. After a game all the reporters crowd round the winner trying to get a quote, but all they get is the same story as every other reporter. Breslin says: "You always go to the losers' dressing room, that's where the story is." That's what made him unique amongst journalists, determined to be different and being willing to put in the effort.

When the story was in the New York tenements, most of the reporters took the lazy way out and interviewed whoever was closest, but Breslin said: "You climb the stairs. All the stories are at the top of the stairs."

This week, do one thing that would make Breslin say: "Good job". Report back on what it was.

#98:

I love live music. Pretty much any genre.

The magic of being in a room full of people and the energy you can feel just before a concert starts.

The performance itself, your favourite songs, the t-shirts from a distant tour, the applause, the freedom to move and to relive a memory. The inevitable encore and the hum of chatter as the audience leaves the venue.

I often thank the artist on social media, showing appreciation for the moment they created. They did a 'good job', but is it right that they command the limelight?

After a recent concert I decided to look deeper beyond the artist on stage. I did some research and produced a gratitude list.

Everyone I could imagine had contributed. From the ticket seller and floor sweeper, through to the lighting designer and amp manufacturer. My list had 120 different roles. All mapped out, all connected and all reliant on each other to deliver the concert I experienced.

I issued a long format 'thank you' letter with everyone mentioned. It got a big response. It helped others to realise the value of a £30 ticket and it has changed the way I appreciate live music forever.

Next time you're watching your favourite band, go and thank the least obvious person in the room. Without them, there's a good chance you and the band wouldn't even be there.

#89:

In a world full of coaches,

I decided to be an anti-coach for the week.

And maybe going forward.

I use opinions. Polarise. Provoke.

I use "Columbo" questions.

"My wife always says..."

"And you think they're going to believe that!"

It's been liberating. Energising.

Sparks. Debate. Emotions.

And new perspectives.

Creativity.

A revelation.

#73:

This question reminded me of one particular client I had late in my journey with my creative agency.

After several initial meetings, where we got to know each other, I asked them deeper questions about their business, their motives, their values, and shared some ideas for how we could work together – and pitched! We agreed on a proposal for work.

The project and relationship went well, and after a few weeks that client said: "I've just realised what you were doing... we thought we were interviewing you and you were pitching to us, **but what was actually happening was that you were interviewing us, and we were pitching to you!"**

I was approached by a potential commissioning client for some consultancy work this week. I haven't yet had the conversation, but I will try to take inspiration from Breslin, and myself!

#25:

Most weeks, I head to some of my clients' offices for a meeting and more often than not, will breeze through reception and get buzzed in.

This week, I decided to do something different.

For every building I went to, I made a point of arriving 10 minutes early to spend that time chatting with someone I wouldn't typically engage with, whether it was the person on the door, a cleaner, a security guard.

My criteria was simply that (1) it had to be someone I wouldn't usually speak to, and (2) I couldn't pull them away from their work (I had no intention of getting anyone fired!).

These brief exchanges, simple yet sincere, gave me a fresh perspective on the places I regularly visit. The little moments, a quick chat about someone's day or a light conversation about their morning, made me realise how much we often overlook, usually because we're in a rush.

So I've made a personal pledge to try and keep doing it. Partly because I enjoy it, and partly because I've probably learnt more than I do from most of the meetings...

Meet the members of Fax Club

What has it been like producing this book?

#06:

Working on this book has been a strong parallel for working on technology products of my past. There's the fuzzy front end where we're finding alignment on direction. A generative and productive creation phase. And that third phase of landing the plane that takes a surprising amount of intentional effort. How do you land the plane? Force of will. There's no autopilot.

It's a real case study in collaboration and dimensional leadership. Different people stepping to the front at different times and then stepping back. A group leading from beside and from behind, willing and wanting to dance.

#48:

Messy, complicated, uplifting, stretching, enlightening, exciting. So many emotions swirling together. It's made me realise I've been a lone wolf most of my working life. I'm used to ploughing on by myself, controlling the pace and direction. Having to collaborate with 30 others? That's been... interesting.

Where do I fit in? Who has what skills? Is anyone leading? Do I hang back or step forward? So many thoughts were spinning in my head. There were moments where it felt overwhelming and then there were moments where I felt such joy at the sheer beauty of people coming together. There was laughter, learning, friendship and a trust that built slowly but surely. We were strangers bound together by a shared challenge and a simple promise to produce a book. On we went, one step at a time.

#03:

It's been a fascinating process, unlike anything I've ever done before. What's really struck me is the loyalty and the bond that's formed between us. I have only the vaguest picture of who everyone really is in practical terms. My knowledge of where some people live ranges from a very broad "the US" to a slightly more specific "Cheshire" or "Cornwall". I know roughly what some people do, but for others I really have no idea. I know for a fact that some people have children or are self-employed or are a specific age, but for many it would be a wild guess. What I do know is how much I trust everyone. I might not know everyone's surname, but there's a common thread to us all. It's hard to put your finger on, but I'd say we're introverted, but passionate; opinionated, but kind. It's those qualities which have got us to where we are now, and kept us going through to publishing this book and beyond.

#80:

I've spent my career working on projects in a different sort of 'publishing' space, where people have a clearly defined role and, other than early-career colleagues, where we're all experts at what we do. Even under those conditions, setting up new projects can be challenging as we form, storm, and norm.

It's been fascinating to witness a group not only learning new skills from scratch, but also figuring out how to self-organise without stepping on each others' toes.

There's been compassion and support for people desperate to lend a hand but struggling to keep up. Miraculous re-injections of energy just when we'd ground to a halt. And a constant flux of people spotting gaps and proactively filling them. I'd love to bottle the commitment for my day job.

Question 33

The robots have arrived

It's 2034. There are as many robots on planet earth as humans. You saw this coming. You robot-proofed your business a decade earlier. What did you do?

#12:

We didn't close the door on the robots. We welcomed them in.

They are helping us to solve some of society's most challenging health, social and environmental problems.

But, back in 2024, we created very clear guidelines on how we would work with robots and we have stuck by them:

1. Separate out the work that requires IQ from the work that requires EQ. Work that requires intelligence (IQ) can be given to a robot with a human in the loop for sanity checking. Work that requires emotional intelligence (EQ) is a human-only task.
2. All robots must identify themselves as such. Any inputs or outputs that have been generated by any form of robot must be labelled as such.
3. Don't work with robots that humans can't fix. If you need a robot to fix your robot then you are on a slippery slope: only work with robots humans can understand.
4. If robots are doing the 'hard' work then humans need to step up and do the 'good' work. And by good we don't mean fun (although fun is good too). We need to be always pushing to make things better for society and for our environment. We can't just sit back and get comfortable with robots doing the work.
5. Only work with robots that are contributing to the solution not becoming part of the problem. Robots we work with

cannot put unnecessary additional pressure on our earth's already fragile resources. Robots we work with need to be enhancing human health and well being not making it worse.

We will be more human. With robots doing many of our daily tasks we will spend the time saved away from technology being more human: we will be out in nature. We will disconnect from technology. We will look after what is around us. We will be wild and connected human beings.

#73:

I launched my 'made slowly by humans' kitemark. A cast iron promise that no robots, no tech, and no devices would be involved during my work with my clients.

So that's not just no robots, but no phones. No computers. No WiFi. No augmented tech. No tech implants.

I started meeting my clients only in totally off grid and natural locations. There wasn't even any electricity! Here, no robots, or tech, or the fruits of their labours could occupy our fields of view. Or our attention.

We'd just relate to each other. And do the work that only humans can do. Where beautiful messy emotive human ideas emerge. Of the sort that only can emerge when two bundles of flesh, bones, hopes and dreams converse with each other.

How special. How unusual. How treasured.

#13:

FAX CLUB

RECIPIENTS: #00-#107

SENDER: #13

SUBJECT: Fax#33

MESSAGE:

It's 2034. There are as many robots on planet earth as humans. You saw this coming. You Robot-proofed your business a decade earlier. What did you do?

A:
I wrote two lists.
The first was all the tedious stuff I hate doing.
The stuff I'm not really good at.
The second was all the stuff I love doing.
The stuff I'm great at.
The first, I gave to the robots.
They're really good at that stuff.
The second, I kept for myself.
I'll always be better at it.
Why? Because I love doing it.
Robots can't do love.

LOVE #13

#38:

I tried to spread love, not fear. I helped the robots see the best side of humanity, by training the AI and the algorithms to emulate us at our highest. The robots have been trained in positive character strengths so they can recognise these strengths in others. The balance is in our hands, humanoids.

#98:

Sorry. This one really stumped me. So I asked a robot for the answer:

I would have future-proofed the business by doubling down on uniquely human traits, developing a culture of creativity, flexibility, and ethical leadership, and by finding a balance between leveraging robotics and emphasising human ingenuity where it matters most.

#49:

I set up a robot spare parts division. Very niche. They come from solar systems near and far for our robot elbows.

#25:

You mean to tell me they got through *this*?!

Question 34

Stop. Stop. Stop.

What three things do you need to stop doing? And why?

#79:

1. **Saying sorry**. I say sorry too much. It's a habit. It's like I'm telling myself I'm wrong, even when I'm not. I'm apologising for things that are out of my control. A bigger problem: I've noticed my daughter doing the same. That's when it hit me. I need to stop. For her. For me. Time to break the cycle.
2. **Paying attention to my limiting beliefs**. Doubt keeps sneaking in, quietly. But it's loud enough to slow me down. It wastes time and energy. It's distracting and takes up space in my head that could be used for something better. These doubts are not facts. They're holding me back from my full potential. Time to move past them.
3. **Holding onto things that don't fit**. I hold on to stuff. Just in case. Maybe I'll need it when I lose weight. Maybe my life will change and I'll use it again. But the truth is, I need to be living for right now. Not my past, not some imagined future. The stuff I hold on to takes up space. Space I need for now. Time to let go.

#42:

1. Worrying. I've taken a conscious leap, uncertainty is guaranteed. Worrying isn't going to get me anywhere. It's what I took the leap to get away from. Worrying is the antithesis of action.
2. Learning. Learning? WTF? Yes, learning is amazing. It's hard to argue with 'learning' IF we're doing something with it. Otherwise it becomes a form of busy-ness. I need to be aware of this trap and lean fully into the 'doing is learning' space.

3. Avoiding sorting out my relationship with my parents. A neighbour dropped dead in front of her (adult) son last week. A stark reminder that you never know when it will be too late. I want to do better for my kids and set an example of what a supportive parent is, which also means I need to show them how adults interact with their parents. That means I need to be the adult that I've never been able to feel like, when I interact with my own, before it's too late.

#89:

1. Trying to force things that don't feel right. Need to listen to my intuition more.
2. Seeing failure as a bad thing. We learn through failure and hardship.
3. Worrying about things I cannot control. This is in response to the quote I love: "Looking back on my life, I have been spending 80% of my time worrying about things that never happened."

#101:

1. Overthinking. It makes me tired.
2. Feeling guilty when taking a rest, as I need to recover and reflect.
3. Taking on too much, it can make me lose focus.

#71:

1. Feeling the pressure of a deadline.
2. Answering things too quickly.
3. Repeating myself.

Why? I don't allow myself the space and the time to be the most creative version of me.

#78:

I need to...

STOP: Trying to do too many things at once! Why? So I can do fewer things better / So I can complete things.

STOP: Scrolling (unless I'm reading Fax Club answers of course!) Why? So I can start properly resting and start making better use of my time.

STOP: Putting my health & fitness last! Why? Well, if I don't start now, when will I start?

#73:

1. **Self-deprecating all over myself.**
   It's a sign of humility, but ultimately leaves others with a strange burden to carry.
2. **Walking up to the edge, but not stepping out over it.**
   It stops others receiving the benefit of my most important work.
3. **Being so invested in what other people may think of me.**
   It usually matters way less to them than it does to me, and reduces my authenticity and impact.

Question 35

The Brain Trust

Pixar had an independent group of people called The Brain Trust. The writers had to get their ideas through it to make the film: "The power of The Brain Trust was that they had no power."

You are about to start a new adventure. You must recruit seven people for your Brain Trust. You can choose anyone. Who are your seven?

#47:

I've decided that my answer to this question must consist of only fictitious characters from children's films, books or TV shows. My seven are...

1. Kevin McAllister for ingenuity
2. Lisa Simpson to be the brains of the operation
3. Animal (Muppet) to maintain team morale
4. Eeyore for black hat thinking
5. Pollyanna to balance the black hat
6. SpongeBob Square Pants the personality hire
7. Superman. Every team needs some eye candy

#38:

1. Richard Feynman
2. #33
3. My older brother
4. My father
5. Frederic Laloux
6. Shane Parrish
7. Maya Angelou

#05:

I have no problem coming up with new ideas for adventures, I'm also a completer finisher, but...

I do set myself up for tough times when I don't have a good plan and people on board to turn my new idea into reality. My Brain Trust will help make sure only my best, most impactful ideas get the focus that they need.

My Brain Trust is made up as follows:

1. My co-founder, and wife, who rarely understands my ideas on first pass, so makes me explain better. She also confidently picks up everything else when I need to complete the job I started.
2. My colleague Liz, who always asks powerful exploratory questions which can help nurture or kill the ideas as appropriate.
3. My youngest adult son, who gets excited when I share ideas and then builds on them with a wide range of impossible possibilities. Often the idea can mushroom or pivot at this point.
4. My friend Paula, who is both a powerful ideation engine herself, but also a realist and anchor to my kite.
5. Our strategic marketing adviser, Su, who can help explore how the idea will land with customers and stakeholders.
6. My first choice IT guru, Dan, who can usually sign-post and support with software and automations to help accelerate most ideas.
7. Lastly, I need to advertise for a post that has been vacant for a while. A political mentor, someone who knows the context in which I operate better than anyone, and can help determine a path of least resistance.

None of the Brain Trust have the power to stop ideas, but collectively they can help the best ideas to flourish!

#80:

The actual people will depend on the adventure. I'd want:

1. Someone who is optimistic, excited and will build further on what we're doing; whose every response is "yes, and... "
2. Someone to challenge our ideas and offer a fresh perspective
3. Someone who will get it done, who rolls their sleeves up and works side-by-side in the trenches
4. Someone who is practical and can figure out how to do almost anything
5. Someone who has intense curiosity
6. Someone who is fearless
7. And finally, someone to cheer us all on when the going gets tough

#88:

I'd go for a mixed group of people and backgrounds who I trust for years, all from different disciplines. From strategists, to neuroscientists, professors, engineers, artists, creatives, musicians, mathematicians and so on...

What an epic mix that would be.

#18:

My wife, my son and daughter, and the remaining slots I'd fill with my mom and siblings (I have a lot of them). My thinking is since it is a non-defined adventure, there is no reason to fill it with outdoor survivalists and genius inventors or the super-rich. Just fill it with people that, in my final breaths, I will regret not having spent more time with, and that is my family.

Question 36

White lies

Under what circumstances is lying OK?

#71:

I have a problematic relationship with disclosure, I seem to see it as binary. Yes or no. All or nothing. And so I default to all: all the details, all the feelings. It's exhausting, overwhelming, like being pressure-washed.

So my answer isn't about lying, it's about discernment. Knowing what to offer and what to keep. All the details are unnecessary and unnecessarily hurtful: that you irritate me with the sound of your cough; that I don't like your new jumper. Choiceful disclosure: the kindest form of truth.

#15:

I've really struggled with this seed. So I thought it best to put it to the back of my mind until such an occasion naturally unfolded. It happened this past weekend at the local pumpkin patch, of all places. There was a bouncy castle which my daughter and her friend were really looking forward to playing on post-pumpkin-picking. The three of us walked over to the cordoned off bouncy castle area where you had to pay to enter. The lady asked if the two girls were five years old, the bar for entry. My daughter had just turned five, her friend was four. I quickly told a white lie and there was a look of knowing between the three of us before they went in to play on the bouncy castle.

#101:

None. But I love this quote from Susan Sontag: "Sanity is a cosy lie."

#11:

When it's the kindest option, and crucially, when knowing the truth wouldn't compromise anyone from making an important decision for themselves.

#32:

I lie to myself daily and it's OK, I encourage myself to do it.

A present lie is a future reality in my mind. This is because I look at myself in the mirror and affirm what I want. The mind is powerful. Lies now, reality later! This is the whole premise of "fake it 'til you make it" and I have seen how effective it can be. Positive lies can affect reality in huge, subconscious ways and completely change your life direction for the better and enhance it.

#47:

I have a friend who tells the funniest anecdotes. Many times, I've been present to witness the events these stories are based on, and the real version never matches the re-telling. Yet, I will take the truth of those circumstances to the grave. The humour his embellishments inject into the story, the glint in his eyes as he tells the tale and the laughter it elicits is worth any damnation I may suffer in the afterlife. Besides, is it really a lie if it's just an omission?

#26:

Only when your kids would be proud of you for it.

Meet the members of Fax Club

Is life after Fax Club any different?

#15:

Yes. I'm attached to an amazing group of people who went through a mad exercise over the course of an even madder year. Our coming together in person for the first time and witnessing the talent and power of our group will stick with me forever. Perhaps Fax Club is only really getting started? I'd like to think so!

#18:

Colors are brighter, sounds are more vibrant. I barely remember life before Fax Club. A better question is whether there is anything that hasn't changed. OK, just kidding. It was a great time and fun to have a larger circle of contacts.

#12:

I miss:

- The excitement of getting the fax on a Friday.
- The anticipation of the question.
- The enjoyment of contemplating an answer over the coming days.
- The process of writing.
- The experience of reading everyone's answers.
- The connection I felt through engaging in conversations around the answers.

#05:

I am thinking broader.

#102:

Absolutely. After a full year of this experience, it's impossible for things to be the same. Seeing everyone in person, feeling the energy turn ideas into action: it was amazing. Just knowing I was part of this magical experiment makes me incredibly happy. I didn't just watch from the sidelines; I jumped in, supported early, and embraced the unknown. It will always be a one-of-a-kind experience, a story I carry with me.

#22:

It's better for having met such amazing people.

#32:

It has taught me the value of pursuing, of continuing despite bumps in the road.

#38:

Yes, I now write and publish things three times a week.
It gave me confidence.

#24:

I miss the Friday anticipation!

#78:

Yes! I've met some lovely people and I hope we can continue to get to know and support each other for years to come. I've never written or published a book, so that's different. There are so many unique people, I think we are the perfect mix to make a success of this (and success will be different for all of us).

Question 37

Silence has the answer

You do a five day silent retreat. What is the one question you want to answer?

#103:

"Who will laugh if I fart really loudly?" They will be my tribe.

#73:

Nothing.

For me, I feel that the purpose of a silent retreat might be to just 'be', not to answer a question. At least, not cognitively.

But after the retreat, I might reflect on the question posed in the poem "The Summer Day" by Mary Oliver: "Tell me, what is it you plan to do with your one wild and precious life?"

#50:

I keep coming up with questions on a theme: "Am I okay?", "Is my child okay?", "Is… everything okay?" But I suppose I know the answer to these, and sitting in silence isn't going to bring much depth or texture to the answer. Maybe what I'm really asking here is something like: "Can I be okay?" Even when it feels like the very next thing will do me in. And maybe the idea of a silent retreat appeals to me not because an answer would come my way, but because I could practice just this task: being okay even when distraction isn't available, and no one is reassuring, and nothing is easy.

#42:

The main question I want to answer is: "Am I on the right path and/or making a difference to anyone?"

It's not particularly big or edifying, except to me at this time of change. I think the reason that this is an elusive question, and probably needs a five day retreat in silence, is that other relatively less pressing questions are crowding my mind, like: What is the Flat Earth movement really about? Why does Quora insist on opening a new tab for every. single. click? And, does my voice sound as weird as I think it does?

#95:

How might the flowing river pass through me,
without getting damned
behind the mound of baggage
being guarded
so keenly
by the lost property attendant within?

Thanks Fax Club, this simple question has brought me to the heart of my biggest challenge!

#47:

What did I do that was so terrible to end up on a five day silent retreat?

Question 38

The pleasure paradox

Is the pursuit of pleasure the pathway to happiness or the surest way to avoid it? Discuss.

#73:

The pursuit of pleasure, to me, is indeed the surest way to avoid true happiness.

I'll try and explain, through a wider frame.

First, I question the pursuit of happiness itself. I'm not being contrary for the sake of it; rather, over the past 10-20 years, I've come to recognise that striving for happiness might be the wrong goal for me. While I can experience happiness in the moment - like when my daughter's laughter fills a room, when I feel a profound connection with others, or when I witness acts of kindness - these moments are fleeting and precious. And they often arise naturally, not through direct pursuit.

Over time, I've observed that the pursuit of happiness has been co-opted, particularly by social media, to fuel consumerism and superficial aspirations. This pursuit creates a perpetual cycle of desire for things we don't need and for personas we long to embody on a surface level. It amplifies feelings of inadequacy or failure when we fall short of constant happiness or aren't 'living our best life.'

For me, this raises a question: is happiness a realistic or credible goal? Can anyone truly be happy all the time? Even when happiness is momentarily 'achieved,' it often proves to be short-lived. It spurs us to set new goals, leading to the unending thought: 'I'll be happy when...' This pursuit can easily morph into a treadmill of temporary satisfaction, never allowing true fulfilment. I believe that striving for a life of perpetual happiness is inherently flawed, at least for me.

As Rick Rubin notes in his book *The Creative Act*: "We can only tell where something is in relation to something else. And we can only assess an object or principle if we have something to compare and contrast it to. Otherwise it's an absolute beyond evaluation."

This resonates deeply with me. Without contrast, how would I recognise happiness? If everything is always hot, how would I know what 'hot' is?

Applying this perspective, it becomes clear that happiness requires contrast to be understood and appreciated. Without moments of sadness, struggle, or even contented neutrality, happiness becomes an undefined, unrecognisable constant.

Over the past 10-20 years, I have shifted my mindset. Instead of aiming for happiness, I have sought contentment.

Contentment is about accepting and experiencing life as it is, where we don't need to be beholden to happiness as a vehicle to a meaningful and nourishing life. It invites us to be surprised and open to what evokes joy or sadness. And to focus on longer-term fulfilment rather than immediate gratification.

So, as paradoxical as it may seem, for me the pursuit of (short-term) pleasure is indeed the surest way to avoid (long-term) happiness.

But beyond that, I've found that happiness itself is not the goal to chase. For me, striving for contentment, regardless of the ups and downs, is the path to a more balanced, fulfilling life. I also recognise that this creates the potential for more experiences of 'happiness'.

#49:

Neither. In my experience, they are two different missions.

Pursuing pleasure is like going for a sugar rush.
Seeking happiness is more like going for a surge of protein energy.

It gets complicated because pleasure can be helpful and unhelpful.

For example, crack cocaine is pleasurable. Unhelpful. Having a massage is pleasurable. Helpful.

Where I think the two missions can come together (but not always) is where something that is a helpful pleasure (exercise, laughter, enjoying a freshly cut piece of orange), can string together for better mood and higher vibes which make openings to happiness.

But then a whoooooole lot more needs to gather for happiness to land.

Both are fleeting.

#12:

Pursue pleasure at your peril.

Pleasure is guilty.
Pleasure is myopic.
Pleasure is insatiable.
Pleasure is a slippery slope.

It will weave its spell and lure you from the pathway to happiness.

If you are intent on pursuing a 'p' may I suggest a few others worth considering...

Play.
Play is creative, collaborative, and challenging.

Passion.
Passion is gritty, sensual, and alive.

Purpose.
Purpose is in it for the long term, fulfilling, clear thinking.

Piquancy.
Piquancy is stimulating, interesting, and exciting.

Choose your 'p' wisely, but I'd advise you to pursue pleasure only at your peril...

#71:

I don't have an answer for this one, I have the two parts of my soul engaged in a full scale brawl.

In the red corner, my impetuous, pleasure-seeking heart following every sniff of adventure and intrigue and possibility. It's sticking two fingers up at the opposition.

In the blue corner, my cool, rational, learned head imploring me to put the brakes on, think things through, consider the consequences and not end up at the "Oh my good god what have I done?" moment. It's shaking its head in despair.

What a glorious contradiction.

The referee seems to be ruling that we've picked the wrong ring to fight over. Happiness isn't the destination. It's something we experience along the way.

As we pause for orange segments we can all agree that a life either full of or empty of pleasure alone is not a healthy way to live.

Balance seems a sanctimonious answer though, so we keep going with the tussle. Everyone's enjoying the punch up. Maybe this is the point?

Question 39

Reverse-engineering success

Think back to one of your biggest successes. Reverse engineer why it went so well. What was the most counterintuitive thing that you did?

#42:

I'm in it at the moment. The counterintuitive thing is not doing what everyone expects.

I am currently challenging myself to change and grow rather than replicate what I know from employment. Despite fear, uncertainty, and doubt, I'm walking my own path and I feel happier than I have in a long time.

The story is being written. It's not even out of Act 1. But it's a new story, not a pastiche (or parody) of something I've read before. And like the best stories, right now, I don't know and can't begin to guess where the hero will end up.

It's a page-turner.

#13:

I was new to leadership, taking over a strong team. Every instinct told me to fake confidence, but I didn't. I admitted I didn't have all the answers. I told them I felt out of my depth, and that I needed their help. That this was our team. Together, we became even stronger. Through showing vulnerability, I became we.

#12:

Looking back on my successes, I'd say there is one thing I did in common across them all.

I worked hard on the preparation and then, in the moment, I let go, secure in the knowledge of my prior work.

#71:

My biggest success in life is my relationship with my stepdaughter. It's hard to put into words how far reaching-ly important and life-changing it has been.

When I think back to how I managed it, these are the steps:

1. I set a clear vision. I knew how I wanted it to be from the start.
2. I took my time and played the long game. There was no pressure.
3. I acted as if it had already happened.
4. I invested loads of time into just being with her.
5. I brought us together through stories, they became our shared history.
6. I documented our love as it grew.
7. I trusted in us both.
8. I enjoyed the ride, even the hard bits gave me something to learn from.
9. I wanted it so badly, but I never demanded it, I knew I had to earn it.
10. I expected nothing in return. Instead, I got everything.

Our relationship has been the defining relationship in my life.

Question 40

The Solomon Paradox

The Solomon Paradox: You are better at giving other people advice, than taking your own. The answer is that you must create distance from yourself and the future you. An easy way to do this is to ask your 85-year-old self for advice. With this in mind, what should you care less about?

#24:

My 85-year-old self would tell me that whilst every day on the outside I will look older, on the inside I become wiser. And like a good book, we judge the contents, not the cover. So, I should spend time learning about my character, purpose and impact and be present in my daily experiences. Because, unlike a book, we don't know when we'll reach the last pages of the final chapter. So let's feel good about the here and now so we don't feel sad when that final sentence comes around.

#32:

Keep doing it, you know what is important. You know your purpose. Keep doing it. Live it. Breathe it. Your time will come.

#18:

Your 85-year-old self would probably remind you to stop sweating the stuff that pulls you off your path, like perfection, comparisons, or fear of failure. Maybe they'd say: 'You were always enough. You were always worthy of love. You didn't need to be anything other than real, true to yourself. Love others as they are. Care less about changing others, but wish for changing yourself to accept them. In other words, remember: bless them, change me.'

#12:

I met my 85-year-old self in the woods.

We walk together, enjoying the autumn sun and the beauty of the woodland. We come to rest on a wooden bench carved out of a fallen tree.

My 85-year-old self thanks me for persistently exercising and doing strength and mobility training so that she can continue to enjoy walks in these woods without concern. I smile.

We talk. We share memories.

I finally pluck up the courage to ask her.
'What should I care less about?'

She turns to me and smiles. She hands me a folded piece of paper. I go to open it, but she says it is for when I get back 'home'.

We walk back through the woods, enjoying the peace and the beauty of the moment.

At home, in my bedroom, I open the paper. In it she has written out the serenity prayer. At first I was confused as I have never followed a specific religion and we didn't talk about religion being part of her life.

But then I sit with the words and I know why she has shared them with me. I put the paper under my pillow and I lock the words into my heart.

What should I care less about? Things I cannot change.

> *God grant me*
> *the serenity to accept the things I cannot change,*
> *the courage to change the things I can, and*
> *the wisdom to know the difference.*

#101:

Stop over thinking the opinion of others.
Stop getting stressed about things that go wrong.

#13:

Everything!
You made 85, dude.
Chill.
The.
Fuck.
Out.

Saying that, don't forget to moisturise.

#103:

Self-doubt.

85-year-old me would say: "Stop giving such a big shit about whether your opinion is valid and interesting and worth speaking. Of course it bloody is!"

I bet it will be so obvious to her.

Question 41

The curiosity budget

The story of our lives is the story of our detours. With this in mind, you have to plan a "curiosity budget" for the coming year. What's the one new thing you want to learn this year?

#103:

Psychedelics. I feel like there's a panel of murky, dirty glass between my conscious and my subconscious mind. I can make out the shapes of some good stuff in there. Stuff that's able to lift some creativity and behaviour blocks, but I can't quite reach it. Despite therapy, coaching and a dedicated creative practice, it's been pushed deeper and deeper into my brain over half a life-time of conditioning.

#49:

Money. From the very beginning.

#22:

I want to learn to play drums.

Four limbs all moving in different directions keeping different time. Turning the frustrations of the day into rhythm not blues.

The vibration of the drum kit reverberating through me; energy creating energy.

The power. The feel. The sound.

The silence that comes in the midst of that noise.

#38:

One new thing! That's going to be my thing. I have too many ideas and want to do too many things at once. I will learn to say "no" and how to decide on the one thing that I am going to focus on for the next year.

#15:

I want to properly understand the carbon footprint of products and services we take for granted; leading towards a much better understanding of the Scope 3 emissions of businesses.

We live in a world full of greenwashing which is substantiated by the continued growth of the planet's CO^2 emissions.

What are we missing? Many businesses lay claim to the emissions reduction path they are on when it comes to their day-to-day operational emissions (Scope 1 and 2). This might be true in many instances but it misses the much bigger picture.

Our deeply damaging status quo will persist until businesses can incentivise and reduce the emissions of their upstream and downstream supply chains, where most of their product or service carbon footprint lies.

I'd like to think we can soon move to a world where citizens are guided in all product / service acquisition decisions by quickly relatable emissions scoring for the choices in front of them.

This already exists in the UK for housing and cars through the EPC rating template. We could apply this recognised graphic much more broadly to better inform decision making in the future.

Question 42

Truths we don't agree on

Entrepreneur and co-founder of PayPal, Peter Thiel, has a favourite interview question: "Tell me something that's true that almost nobody agrees with you on?"

What's your answer?

#79:

Motherhood fuels ambition.

They said you can't have it all.
They were wrong.

Motherhood gave me more than I ever imagined.

A stronger sense of self.
Inspiration for my creativity.
Clarity on what truly matters.
A feeling of belonging.

Life is harder but more rewarding.
Chaotic, but full of purpose.
Changed, but for the better.
Time is short, but it's well spent.

Aiming higher.
Striving for better.

For them and for me.
That changes everything.

"Motherhood is the greatest thing and the hardest thing." Ricki Lake

#88:

All weather is beautiful (even rain), you just need to dress for it.

#25:

My truth: *Being 'right' doesn't matter; being convincing does.*

The power of persuasion lies not in truth, but in resonance. We don't act based on facts alone; we act on feelings, narratives, and connection. In leadership, being 'right' is a static state, useful, but lifeless. Conviction, however, is dynamic. It transforms data into meaning, inspiring others to believe and act.

Think about the movements and ideas that changed the world. They didn't thrive because they were objectively correct; they thrived because they were compelling, human, and relatable. Truth may be universal, but the story is personal, and that's what changes minds.

#98:

The human race is obsessed with collecting material possessions rather than memories. We make excuses for ourselves, but our consumption is often unnecessary and unsustainable.

I'm guilty. I fell into the social norm. Seeking a better car, a bigger house and mobile phone with more apps than I'll ever use.

It felt like progress. Everyone around me was embarking on the capitalist staircase of life. However, there is an alternative way.

I set myself the task of listing every item in my house that wasn't required on a daily basis. Excluding personal items such as photos and artwork, the list had hundreds of entries. It shocked me.

I then listed my most cherished moments and memories over the last month. The list was shorter and filled with people, places, interactions, stories and laughter. It didn't feature any of those non-essential objects. It was only joy.

So, next time you're about to purchase something you don't truly need, stop. Select a memory instead. Write it down, relive it, and treat it as a mind transaction. It's one of the most important investments you can make.

Your house will be emptier and your life will be fuller.

Meet the members of Fax Club

What does Fax Club mean to you in three words?

#38:

Freedom to be.

#102:

Spark. Challenge. Magic.

#13:

Clarity. Focus. Direction.

#03:

Brave. Creative. Expanding.

#78:

Connection. Evolving. Unique.

#15:

Brilliantly mad connections.

#22:

A unique experience.

Question 43

Walk in their shoes

For one week, take the opposite view to one of your beliefs or worldviews. Read only their media. Listen only to their podcasts. Make only their arguments. Walk in their shoes and try to understand why they think this way.

#73:

I do quite a bit of this already as I feel it's absolutely crucial in these polarising times to have empathy for what has led people to believe the things, or to act in the way that they do.

It was super hard to go deeper though. I felt my skin crawl and my brain ache. My emotions felt extreme. And through that exercise I have learned that that is part of the problem in the world.

I pride myself in listening. In 'leaning in', in trying to see the world through the eyes of others. But I still often listen to what I want to hear or agree with. Not in a truly open way to have my mind open to change. And no matter how hard I try, my conscious or unconscious biases play a significant role.

And here is the problem. I feel that I am open, but I wonder how open I actually am? Which points to even more work to be done. Thank you for this one.

#12:

"Belonging is an ambiguous state, you know. Take this place, for example. We can both be in the same place, but having that sheet of glass between us makes us feel as if what is happening on the other side is irrelevant, doesn't it? Remove the partition, however, and instantly you become part of the same world. Even though it is all one to begin with."
What you are looking for is in the library by Michiko Aoyama.

This passage jumped out at me as I was contemplating this week's fax question.

The concept of belonging as an ambiguous state, something fluid rather than absolute. That is the true state of belonging.

Because we all change.

We develop different interests and move to different places.

Our lives aren't fixed, and neither is our worldview.

But implicit in this week's question is an assumption of absolutes: 'their media', 'their podcasts'. It is 'us' vs 'them'.

It seems that the fluid nature of belonging and our ability to remove the glass that separates us is something that society has forgotten.

But why?

What I found when trying to complete this week's challenge may go someway to answering that question.

My first task was to find the 'media', 'podcasts' and 'arguments' from those with a different worldview to my own. I attempted a Google search, but found I was presented back with pieces written by people with my worldview talking about people with a different worldview (and why they are wrong).

I spent a while scrolling social media and found much the same. I even took a look on my podcast app, but wasn't sure what to search for.

I tried asking ChatGPT. But it just shared a summary of the 'opposing view' which felt factual and dull. There was no nuance, no emotion, no understanding.

Even when I tried to find the opposing view I couldn't get out of my own echo chamber.

The algorithms said no.

And it is the algorithms that are driving us apart. It is the algorithms that are putting up more and more sheets of glass between us. Or more specifically it is the companies behind the algorithms.

Because polarisation creates emotion > emotion draws attention > attention can be monetised > and money gets companies rich.

So thanks to the algorithms I didn't get a chance to walk in 'their' shoes. But if I did I expect they would feel much the same as mine, we walk on the same earth after all. But I'm pretty sure their echo chamber would sound very different.

So until we fight the algorithms there are just going to be more and more sheets of glass placed between us, and even those who are willing to try, will find it very hard to smash through.

#22:

I haven't watched the news for over 10 years.

During that time, I've been called ignorant. I've even questioned myself as to whether I'm burying my head in the sand.

But without news the quality of my life has been much better. I've felt generally more positive, less fearful, and more hopeful about the world because I've defined it by MY world and not the one forced upon me by mainstream media.

This week I watched and listened to the news on the TV and radio.

All I can say is that I won't be doing it again. Dark, depressing, fear-mongering, divisive. I felt heavier, darker, more fearful and less hopeful.

#47:

Looking at the world through the eyes of another is difficult, and with the objective of learning about others, I actually learned more about myself and the values that define one of my core beliefs. Sometimes the best way to find out what you do believe in is by identifying what you don't.

I chose to investigate the world of the tradwife: a world where women embrace traditional gender roles, focusing on being a wife, a mother, and a homemaker. I fully support the right of any woman to live however she pleases and have no issues with this lifestyle choice. It was fascinating to peek inside this world and marvel at the women who make every meal from scratch and maintain immaculately clean and tidy homes. I can absolutely understand the appeal of this lifestyle and even picked up a few new recipes and cleaning life hacks along the way.

However, my struggles began when I encountered a subset of tradwives who advocate for this lifestyle as the only acceptable one for women. This challenged and surfaced a core belief that I hadn't consciously recognised until now: that everyone, regardless of gender, has the right to live life as they choose, but no one has the right to impose their choices on others.

Criticising women who prioritise their careers or implying that they're 'less than' because they don't put their husband's needs above their own is something I cannot accept. To me, this is not a matter of narrow-mindedness but of principle.

Exploring the tradwife world taught me a valuable lesson, not just about others, but also about myself. While I can appreciate the appeal of this lifestyle and celebrate the freedom that allows women to choose it, I remain steadfast in my belief that there is no single path to living a fulfilling and meaningful life. True empowerment comes not from conformity to one ideal but from embracing the diversity of choices that life offers.

Question 44

My chemical gratitude

Expressing gratitude is scientifically proven to make you feel happier.

Write a letter to the person who influenced you the most. Describe how you feel about them. Now call them and read out what you wrote.

What happened? Did science get it right?

#22:

I was at a stuffy, posh grammar school. It made Hogwarts look like Grange Hill.

It was a very academic school. I wasn't very academic, I was creative but I didn't appreciate that yet, so they thought I was a rebel and I thought I was stupid.

And then, in the fourth year, a young art teacher started, Mr McGuinness. He saw me. He saw something in me, and he nurtured it, encouraged it. I came alive.

He taught me about art history and introduced me to David Hockney and Mondrian. I fell in love with them. He was into cool music too. He told me about a band he was friendly with, Half Man Half Biscuit. I thought it was the best name for a band I had ever heard. I fell in love with them. I got an A in GCSE graphic design.

And then I left school, but I always followed my creative urges, thanks to Mr McGuinness, but I never said thank you.

A few years ago, 30 years later, I found him online and so I wrote to him and told him how he had changed my life. He was surprised and a little embarrassed. He had given up teaching not long after he taught me. He didn't think he was cut out for it.

I was happy that I had let him know how important he had been in my life, but I was sad that I hadn't told him earlier. Maybe he would still be a teacher.

I asked him what he was up to now, but his reply was short and sweet. He had to dash to go and pick his kids up from school. I figured his life had turned out pretty good then.

His kids are lucky, they've got a cool dad. No doubt he plays Half Man Half Biscuit to them.

#12:

On first consideration of this question, my default thinking led me to interpret 'influenced' as 'inspired'. I was mentally running through the people that have inspired me when it struck me.

The person, or I should say people, that have influenced me the most aren't those that I put on a pedestal and admire from afar. No, they are the people that are with me every single day, they are my children.

My children have influenced...

Where I live.
The work that I do.
What time I wake up.
The pattern of my day.
What makes me happy.
What makes me scared.
My purpose.

What is interesting about this type of influence is that sometimes it can produce feelings of resentment rather than gratitude.

But in writing my letter, I was grateful.

Grateful for every single choice that my children have influenced. Grateful for our time together, no matter how hectic it may feel. Grateful for all the lessons they have taught me.

Because without them I wouldn't be me.

I didn't read them my letter. It might be something I will share with them when they are older. But I did hug and kiss each one and thanked them for making me their mum. The littlest asked me "what do you mean?" and the middle and oldest gave me a weird look and carried on with what they were doing.

But as far as the science goes: yes, that did make me feel happier. Thank you, science.

#89:

I help my son, who is 14, for school. He has ADHD and struggles with the rigidity of the school system. Its rules, its long tests throughout the year, the pressure it puts on him.

Being in a transition phase in my professional life, the fact that I help him - with the preparation, the consistency, and the discipline - is giving me purpose and the structure that I currently need.

I wrote him a short (he's part of the TikTok generation) letter to thank him for everything he is giving me at this point in time. We're in this together, learning loads about ourselves and each other. Growing through the process.

It felt good to say it. To write it down.

#88:

I had to write a letter I can't read out anymore or call them as they died from suicide over a year ago. I am forever grateful for him and the 12 years I've known him.

If you're reading this, dear friends, call that person and tell them how you feel.

Question 45

The year of nothing new

You have now gone over a year without buying anything new. What will be the first thing you buy? And why that?

#15:

A wooden surfboard making course.

An experience providing skills whose outcome is a much loved product commencing a life of its own through shared joy.

Just the other morning, I was sitting at dawn on my one-and-only surfboard purchased twenty four years ago. The pink glow of the early morning light and the reflections off the water were indescribably beautiful. I found it impossible not to reminisce about the places we'd been together and the waves we both glided upon.

However, I also thought about the next twenty four years and wondered if at sixty six I'd still have the power in my arms to stroke the same board into similar waves early enough to pop up and set the trim.

Which got me thinking about building a wooden longboard that would allow a little more time for all elements to combine. There's a timeless quality to wood and the roots of surfing are completely intertwined.

I can only imagine what it would feel like to catch your first wave on a wooden surfboard you've built with your bare hands.

One day.

#49:

A present for my husband. Something small and thoughtful and useful. Carefully wrapped with a card with just a few words on it.

#05:

I do try not to buy anything unless I need it. I have a 35 year old surf board, a 19 year old mountain bike, a 15 year old Patagonia coat.

If I bought nothing new for a year then the first thing I would buy is a pair of Adidas Terrex walking shoes. I know these last me about a year, so I will need a new pair by then.

I know this as I have been experimenting with footwear over the last four years as I walk my dog for 10,000 steps every day. I don't want to wear chunky hiking boots throughout the year so go for trail shoes. The only brand I have found that has a sole that lasts over six months are the Adidas Terrex.

#20:

A sewing machine. Because I'd like to continue to not buy any new clothes or soft furnishings at least. I can repair and reimagine existing pieces over and over again with a sewing machine.

#103:

It has to be a book. Or a Derwent Inktense pencil. These are the things I will miss the absolute most. Books are how I make sense of what I think. Pencils are how I make sense of what I see.

(Question: Does it count if I've raided World of Books and Cass Art before the Year of Nothing New starts?)

Question 46

The thorn in your side

I have a splinter in my hand. One way to get it out is to get a needle, eek.

But there is another, more counterintuitive, way. Cover it with a plaster, and over days, the skin softens and the splinter is much easier to get out. What in your life or business could benefit from thinking "more plaster"?

#05:

The plaster is a metaphor for softening something up by getting close to it, supporting it, protecting it. My business is all about engaging other businesses, so relationships are key, and these definitely need a 'plaster' approach. The needle equivalent in relationship building is the pitch-slapping we receive on LinkedIn or at networking events. Rarely works, or makes a mess.

I can build more, and better, relationships by taking the plaster approach:

- Covering = asking open questions and getting to know people.
- Supporting = seeking to add value first before getting value. Be likeable.
- Softening = building the relationship as a person so that business can be done. Building trust.

We need more plasters!

#26:

Every goddamn moment someone winds me up with a stupid comment. Take a breather. Let the skin soften. Be more plaster.

#13:

FAX
CLUB

RECIPIENTS: #00-#107

SENDER: #13

SUBJECT: Fax#46

MESSAGE:

What in your life or business that could benefit from thinking more plaster?

A:
Creating the appropriate response.
It might be a situation that tests your composure,
A delicate issue that demands a cool head,
Or an unpopular decision that needs to be shared.

How we respond to any given situation,
Is the only thing we truly control.

A pointed approach taken in haste can cause harm,
Potentially causing long-term damage.
Sometimes, it's better to soften the approach:
Put a plaster on it and take the sting out.

LOVE #13

#12:

When emotions are high it is all too easy to respond in the moment, immediately jabbing at the situation with our needle.

But in the wise words of Viktor Frankl:

"Between stimulus and response there is a space. In that space is our power to choose our response. In our response lies our growth and our happiness."

So when a situation provokes a heightened emotional response, I try to apply a plaster, because a plaster increases the space between the stimulus and response.

In that space feelings cool and time opens up, allowing us to consider different responses. We can then make a choice, and our response may not be the same as the one we would have taken in the moment.

I have recently been involved in some rather tricky contract negotiations. Money is involved, and egos. Discussions in person become heated and emails are terse. However, we have all chosen to take the plaster approach. We aren't insisting that 'this is resolved right now', and have instead said 'before the new year'. We have chosen to sit with the discomfort of an unresolved situation. In doing so we have given ourselves the space to think through all the points of view and to make a choice about our response, with the knowledge that it is in this response that our growth and happiness lie.

#25:

This feels like a good analogy for the quest for "creativity."

I feel like a lot of people in my sphere treat inspiration like a splinter: they grab a needle and start digging, grinding through late nights and blank pages in the hope that sheer effort will shake something loose.

It rarely does.

I've inadvertently stumbled into a more "plaster method" approach. I step away; let the problem marinate. Go for a walk, fold some laundry, or stare aimlessly out of a window like a poet in a 19th-century novel.

Creativity has a habit of working itself out when you're not paying attention, usually in the shower, mid-jog, or in the depths of the night.

It turns out, the best ideas don't come when you're forcing them; they arrive when you've tricked your brain into thinking it's off-duty.

#47:

My father tells a story about the night he got lost in Marrakesh. Separated from his friends and alone in an unfamiliar city, he couldn't remember the way back to the youth hostel. Mild frustration turned to panic, then fear, as it dawned on him that all his money, belongings and passport were at the hostel. Eventually, he resigned himself to the situation and sat down on a pile of sand at a nearby building site. As the sun rose, he recognised where he was and easily made his way back to the hostel. Sometimes, if you don't know what to do, you just need to sit on a pile of sand and wait for the way forward to become clear.

#22:

I would benefit being more plaster when it comes to my kids.

I can't bear seeing them suffer in any way, so when they come to me with something they are struggling with, I want to fix it for them, advise them, make it better, and take their pain away.

But, I know it's an important part of their growth to overcome their own challenges.

Taking the plaster approach, I can support and encourage whilst patiently standing by as the splinter works its way out for them.

Meet the members of Fax Club

Did you follow the rules?

#74:

I can now share that I answered some of the questions late… and I even skipped a few of them.

This allowed me to experience:

1. The concept of 'binge-writing': sitting for an hour with a beer, tackling one, two, even three questions in a row to get it done, and then accepting that it wasn't perfect.
2. Done is better than perfect.
3. The power of the collective. I was absolutely impressed by some of the contributions. Thanks for the examples guys. Awesome!

#24:

My husband needs a shout out here. He spent hours working out how to get me a working fax machine!

#48:

At the beginning, I found it fascinating to watch everyone find their way in a space with very little rules, complete anonymity and no leader. Some numbers were seeking more clarity. Word count limits, deadlines and voting options were all things discussed in the chat. I remember early on wondering if it was all a game. Was this even real? Were the questions a ruse and the real experiment was seeing what happens when you put 100 people together in a space with limited rules?

#14:

I broke the rules, I'm a maverick pirate, rules are there to be broken! I missed multiple deadlines. I missed some answers. I did tell a couple of people about Fax Club. They were intrigued, bemused and in awe of the challenge.

I did use a fax machine and revelled in it whirring into action every Friday night! I miss the sound.

#15:

I took the rules very literally. No one knew that I was part of Fax Club until the day after we all met in London. My young family live in a small bungalow in rural South Devon and I quickly became entirely reliant on other Fax Clubbers sharing the questions each week because it was going to take an age to have an additional telephone line installed. I'd stupidly, in hindsight, submitted our home telephone number and every Friday afternoon the phone would ring with a fax tone!

#05:

I told my wife I was doing Fax Club. She thought it was weird, but knew I would enjoy it.

#03:

I told my husband, but no one else. I think he thought it's possibly another thing I didn't need to take on, particularly when we were on holiday and I spent a day on the beach furiously typing into the notes function in my phone as it felt like a good moment to catch up with unanswered questions! I refer to it as "my Fax thing" and I know he thinks it's strange, but he just lets me get on with it and has seen I've got a lot of joy out of it.

Question 47

Shared beliefs, shared limitations

A 1971 essay by Murray S. Davis called 'That's Interesting' explains what gets attention, and why a counterintuitive method can be so powerful. After reading it, ask yourself: "What's a popular truth in my industry that's secretly holding everyone back?"

#98:

Collaboration not competition.

People are obsessed with the competition. What are they doing? Why did they make that decision? How did they get those results? And, most importantly, how can we get ahead of their next move?

Yes, competition can be a motivator. But it's also a distraction. Focus on competitors can halt your founder's mindset and drain energy from your own work. Jealousy can easily lead to anxiety and continued comparison kills creativity

Instead, channel that energy into collaboration. Distribute your ideas. Share your biggest mistakes and drive your industry forward with combined efforts.

Some of the greatest human achievements have arisen when collective action is taken and differences are put aside.

So why not bring your biggest competitors closer? Do that, and you won't just keep up, you'll stand out.

#48:

I'm fascinated by the 'Good Mother' myth, the belief that maternal self-sacrifice equals good parenting. This widely-accepted 'truth' reinforced by society is actually limiting our children's potential. When mothers (or fathers) suppress their own dreams and identity in the name of selfless parenting, they unconsciously teach their children to do the same.

Ask most parents what they want for their children, and they'll say 'happiness.' But how can our children truly learn true happiness if we're not modelling it authentically? Not the superficial kind, but the deep lasting fulfilment that comes from living in alignment with our values and pursuing our dreams.

The most powerful gift we can give our children isn't endless self-sacrifice, it's showing them what it looks like to live fully while loving deeply.

#25:

The popular "truth" that so many worship in my industry is the adage 'if you can't measure it, it doesn't matter.'

On paper, it sounds wonderfully sensible, but in practice, it's holding us hostage. The best ideas, the ones that genuinely change hearts, minds, and markets, often refuse to squeeze themselves neatly into a spreadsheet.

Inspiration doesn't come with a bar chart, and emotional connection rarely submits to a tidy ROI.

Yet we chase metrics like moths to a flame, ignoring the fact that the most powerful magic in business, trust, curiosity, loyalty, can't be quantified.

By obsessing over what's measurable, we risk overlooking the immeasurable moments that make people truly care.

#47:

The popular belief that "feedback is a gift" is utter bollocks. It might be a gift, but in my opinion, the best gifts come with a receipt, so you can exchange them if they're not right for you.

I'm not saying you should ignore all feedback, but let's be honest: plenty of it hides behind murky excuses like "I'm just being honest" or "I tell it how I see it". As if those phrases somehow excuse unkind, unhelpful, or downright hurtful comments. Just because something is labelled as feedback doesn't mean it's accurate, useful, or even worth your time.

Ask yourself:

1. **Who gave it to you?** Not all feedback-givers are equally insightful, or equally relevant. I'd even go so far to suggest that some are unqualified to provide feedback.
2. **Why did they give it to you?** Is their intent to help you grow, improve, and shine? Or is it to dim your light and plant seeds of doubt?
3. **What's in it for them?** Does this feedback serve their interests in some way? Why are they offering it now? Timing and motivation matter.
4. **How does it benefit you?** Does this feedback genuinely help you improve, or does it just create unnecessary turmoil?

I'm not saying you should dismiss anything negative and only embrace the positive. Home truths can be hard to hear but incredibly valuable when they're constructive and well intentioned. What I am saying is that not all feedback is worth taking to heart. So before you swallow it whole, take a moment to examine it first.

Question 48

Small experiment, big idea

It's the week between Christmas and New Year when, for many, the normal order takes a pause. What's the smallest experiment you can run this week to test a big idea while you enjoy the break?

#89:

Loving people I actually don't necessarily like and patiently trying to understand their context, stories and perspective.

#12:

This week I have been lost in the land of Carlo Rovelli's ideas.

I picked up his book *White Holes* in a bookshop whilst looking for some good 'Twixmas' reads. I flicked to the opening page and read these lines:

"Beginning is the hardest step. The first words open a space. Like the first glance of the girl I am about to fall in love with - a life is decided by the hint of a smile."

These are the first lines of a book written by a theoretical physicist describing his findings about White Holes, the younger siblings of Black Holes.

Wow!

For the past few days I have been mesmerised by Rovelli's words and by his ideas, he takes the reader on a journey into a White Hole, a place where time and space melt. But the thing I find most fascinating is not his explanation of White Holes (although they are totally mind-blowing) but it is the frequency with which he uses the word 'beautiful' to describe mathematical concepts and how Rovelli uses literary references to bring to life scientific and mathematical concepts. What becomes clear is that he isn't the only one to write and think about science in this way, through his overview of the great thinkers whose revelations led to our current understanding of the relativity of time, Rovelli shares how these great thinkers made huge leaps in our understanding not because they were brilliant at maths and science (although they were), but because they were curious about lots of diverse things. They loved art and nature and maths and science. And when they thought about the Earth and Space, they brought their multiple passions together and were able to intuit things that were beyond the realms of the collective imagination.

So for me a small experiment is to once a month (in the words of another great and tragic theoretical physicist Karl Schwarzschild) 'walk in the land' of another's ideas.

The more diverse the better.

The big idea is that the biggest leaps come from joining the dots between diverse and seemingly unrelated concepts.

So here is to a new year full of meandering explorations and some big, crazy ideas.

#50:

My big idea is that maybe I can be a writer, even during this time of my life when I feel stretched thin and like I don't have enough time for... anything. A wiser part of me thinks this idea that I don't have enough time is just... a bad idea. A protective little thought. An... excuse? I'd like to get over that this year, nurture a different thought. The smallest experiment I could think of to do this week... well, write. I suppose I'm doing that now. And then don't get hung up on the other stuff, when will I write again, what is my ideal schedule, what am I even doing? Just... ten minutes of writing a day. Before the big leap into living a new idea.

#25:

This week, I've been making a point to weave a subtle, genuine compliment into every conversation I have.

Not the usual "I like your shoes" variety, but something that feels both thoughtful and specific. Like telling a colleague their sense of humour makes working between Christmas and New Year worth it; or noticing how someone's perspective shifted the way I saw a problem; or even thanking my uncle for the way he manages to bring up politics at Christmas dinner without completely ruining the pudding.

So far, the results have been intriguing.

Conversations feel less transactional, more open. There's this subtle but noticeable shift, as if people lean in just a little closer, respond just a bit more openly. The surprising thing is how it's changed me. Instead of autopilot conversations, I'm actively looking for what I genuinely admire in others.

It's not just about saying something nice; it's about noticing.

The real magic, though, is how effortless it feels.

A single sentence, well-placed, has the power to transform a fleeting interaction into something more human. I'm halfway through the week, and while I can't measure the long-term ripple effect, I can already tell this experiment is sticking around. It's made every interaction feel just a little bit brighter.

And that, in itself, feels like a win.

Question 49

More fool us

Penn & Teller, the renowned magician duo, are known for their innovative and often unconventional magic tricks. One such trick involves a unique card revelation at a cemetery.

They get you to pick a card, and then the magicians lead you to the cemetery.

There, they find the grave inscribed with the words: "Is this your card?", along with an image of the Three of Clubs: the card you picked.

The easy bit was getting you to pick the right card.

The hard bit was getting permission from the graveyard, getting it inscribed, and waiting for the grass to grow over.

"Sometimes magic is just someone spending more time on something than anyone else might reasonably expect."

How can you apply the principle of investing disproportionate effort behind the scenes to create magic in your work or projects in the coming year?

#12:

Late one Sunday evening my co-founder sent me this message, "I will cherish the pictures of you using a Spiderman ruler to measure the logo on a mug we have stolen."

We had been debating the size, colour, and placement of our logo on some promotional mugs for over a week. These debates often happen at strange hours. I would message at 6am comparing the size of logos, he would reply at midnight invariably asking me to explore further, and on and on we went for days.

This is because we felt that it was important. Important to sweat the small stuff. Because details matter.

In his message my co-founder had said “a mug we have stolen”, and yes, I'm sorry to admit we had each stolen a mug from the Alan Turing Institute. We stole them because we thought they were cool. That is marketing in action.

Richard Branson had the bottom of Virgin Atlantic's Upper-Class salt and pepper shakers embossed with the wording “I stole this from Virgin Atlantic”.

He understood the power of marketing.

We aspire to have our mugs stolen, and this is why we continued to debate logo size and placement into the wee small hours.

So my resolution for the coming year is to continue to sweat the small stuff, because it is in the small details that the magic happens.

#89:

Japan is filled with tiny, extraordinary businesses that strive for perfection. A little café, a minuscule sushi restaurant, a boutique flower shop.

The principle behind this is called “Kodawari”, which is a personal standard to which someone adheres completely, understood as a very high level of quality or professionalism.

This is often applied as a lifelong process, keeping in mind that life needs evolution and growth, not revolution. It explains the phenomenal level of customer service in Japan.

If we apply Kodawari to the activities we love, we can create magic this year and far beyond.

#88:

Continue to nurture relationships and prioritise connections; the juice in life that has always created magic.

#98:

I turn 50 years old this year. The age doesn't bother me, but the number is important to me.

Why?

Well, on my 25th birthday I decided to write a vision for my future self. I wanted it to feel like a stretch. A dream that could be fulfilled through hard work and a story that I would re-visit 25 years later on my 50th birthday.

At the age of 25 I had started my career, but the transition from university to work hit me hard. Loneliness entered my life as friends relocated, anxiety began to dominate my emotions and ill health became my baseline.

I didn't want this to be my future. So I created a 'framework to thrive'. I used to refer to it as 'Bob'. That way, the character became an excuse to spend time with someone that nobody would question and that nobody would ever meet.

Effort became my best friend, my councillor and my medicine. It took commitment and bravery. It needed research and required trust. It resulted in more failures than successes. But slowly, all of the effort was helping me to change the hand of cards that I'd been dealt back in my 25th year.

How do I apply this principle in my work today?

I remember that the true magic lies in the human reaction and not the trick itself. My dream for a better future only became reality because I made it happen.

So, I do something every day that requires effort. Effort that I know I will thank myself for in another 25 years.

Oh... and thanks to Bob, I am now thriving!

#103:

My instinct and nature used to be to do this:

To wallow and bathe in the slow and delicious process of creation. But I have allowed this instinct to be beaten out of me.

How hard it is to call it back into play!

I am a creative.

I won't be making amazing work if I am always creating in a rush.

I hereby give myself permission, from this year onwards, to wallow, luxuriously in my creative process.

The results will have more authenticity and garner more respect.

#32:

This is literally how I live my life. I am a musician and mix engineer. My life is inundated with potential client meetings, the expectation of doing highly skilled work for exposure and chronically thinking about how best to market myself and music.

However I have a relentless faith in the quality of my work and my purpose that I keep on. I keep on every. single. day working on my craft in the studio. It is very isolating at times. Often people talk about AI and its implications for the music and artistic industries however I think someone spending hours on their craft will become even more valuable and sought for, like a needle in a haystack.

People, especially the younger generation are moving towards analogue, virtuosity and away from cheap sounds. This brings me hope, I continue (I would anyway regardless). Virtuosity is not something you can fake on a surface level: people hear it.

Question 50

Building different

Everyone is talking about AI agents, but all those people who are talking about AI agents have one thing in common: They are not building an AI agent.

At Fax Club, we think different because we do different.

We build, they talk. And because we build, we learn what the future will be like before it arrives. We understand it because we took an afternoon to build it.

By building, we get a sneak peek into what's coming, an understanding that talking alone can never provide.

It's time to build.

#25:

I've been back and forth on the idea of AI for some time now and, truth be told, still don't know quite where I land.

I wonder if the true power of building AI isn't actually efficiency, but how it creates the freedom to be delightfully inefficient.

Hear me out.

Paradoxically, this is where the most valuable human creativity resides. So what if we built to reclaim back time for the things that make us human? To make space for curiosity to run wild, unhindered by tasks AI can handle better?

The act of building isn't just about creating tools; it's about designing the conditions for serendipity and letting machines optimise so we can rediscover the joy and ingenuity of simply being human.

#06:

You've been standing at the bus stop waiting.

35 minutes in already, the bus is 12 minutes late.
You say, "I'll give it five more minutes."

Seven minutes later what do you do?

Dilemma?

In a world full of distraction, attention is a commodity.
Am I squandering my attention? Or applying it with focus to create impact. The intentional channelling of attention toward a cause.

Purpose.

To decide.

To cut away choice.
All the shiny things vying for our finite attention.
Nothing shines brighter for an ex-software engineer than new tech.

And so down the rabbit hole I went.

Two days, too much or too little?

Quick-start guides that are out of date.
Not tested on my set-up.
No high-level overview.

Homebrew? npm, or pnpm? Bash or zsh?

I was so close.
Got an agent running.
I said hello.

50,000 words of red error text in the console.
Verbose logging enabled.

Ah, I have to pay for LLM models.
More choice.
I'll go back to ChatGPT. Two hours training it on my writing.

Ohhhhh.
Now I see something interesting.
Maybe.

I'll give the bus five more minutes.

#79:

I had trouble understanding the question. So I turned to ChatGPT.

Its answer was all about taking action and it inspired me to write this.

We're taught to learn before doing.
But maybe we learn best by doing first.
Doing helps us understand.
Doing helps us play.
Doing helps us learn.
Collaboration (something I wasn't taught at school) takes it to the next level.
Building on others' ideas.
Taking doing even further.
I'm not waiting for someone else to create this.
I'm starting a community.
Locally. Face to face.
Offline. No algorithms deciding who we meet.
Exchanging challenges. Building ideas.
Asking questions. Passing on knowledge.

Together, creating, building.
Something bigger than ourselves.
A sneak peek into the future.

Back to AI.
We think AI is taking us further online.
But maybe it's leading us back to each other.
I've been thinking about building a GPT.
Maybe I just need to DO IT!

I'm still not sure if I answered the question right, but it did get me thinking.

I also found this quote that I found profound:

"We shape our tools, and thereafter our tools shape us."
Father John Culkin (but often attributed to Marshall McLuhan)

#103:

Full disclosure here: there's not one part of this that attracts me. I spend my life trying to get off a screen in order to do the analogue things that fill me with purpose and actually drive my work forward. (And when work finishes, I spend my life trying to get my kids off screens). Life needs to slow the heck down, not speed the heck up. Productivity pressure needs to properly bog off too.

For me, learning to build an AI agent would be on a par with sticking pins in my eyes.

Perhaps that's narrow-minded. Or selfish. And maybe I'll fall behind, but I don't care. 'Online' is 'overwhelm' to me, and it rattles my brain. For that reason, I only ever plan to use the bare bones of what a screen can offer me.

(I still have never looked at ChatGPT. I never plan to either.)

POSTSCRIPT:
If I had to choose between an AI agent built by someone in Silicon Valley, or an indie-entrepreneur based in Wales, it's obviously a no-brainer. However, architecting some just really AI ain't for me.

POST POSTSCRIPT:
I also can't get behind the environmental footprint of running so many servers for AI.

Question 51

The questions that made you truly think

Now a moment of reflection. Of all the questions that have been asked, which one really made you think the most and why?

#98:

Fax #44 made me think the most.

It suddenly opened my eyes. Demonstrating to me how easy it was to turn writing into action. An action that reconnected with my past to influence my future.

Recognition and thanks in its simplest form has a big impact. It highlights the complexity and joy of one human spirit influencing another human's life. There is something truly magical in that.

The gift of a question has changed my life forever. The power of simple words to transform the complex world around you.

#78:

The question that made me think the most (apart from this one) was Fax #25!

I loved spending the time to think, to get creative and to write it down. It made me think the most as the founder / owner is a friend of mine and I would love to help her succeed!

I also love that I got a very sweet reply.

#06:

The question that really made me think the most and why? This one of course!

It invites me to reflect on 50 brilliant conversations and asks me to pick just one. The one that made me think the most.

In revisiting these 50 questions I've paid attention to what they created within me:

- One was wonderfully playful and held me in exquisite creativity.
- One was challenging, a powerful reminder of something important that I sit with often.
- Two were uncomfortable, scary, and ultimately insightful.
- One was wonderfully enjoyable, it took me back to being a student.
- One posed a provocative six word question that set my brain somersaulting.
- One invited boldness outside my comfort zone.
- Two offered such rich and fertile metaphors.
- Two I had no knowledge to access, and seem important for us all.

By inviting me to review my experiences and go through this body of work we've built up, without doubt, this question has had me think the most.

And this seems perfect. If we are to surface learning we need both action and reflection.

50 questions in, well there's been plenty of action.

And now a constructed space for reflection.

#38:

All of the questions made me show up in a new way. Every time I answered I gained something in the form of a little bit more confidence to get a rebellious view out there. The support of anonymous hands represented a safe environment in which to express with total honesty.

And now I cannot wait to meet you all!

The questions that also educated me were the most powerful. I felt like they were spiritual; new ways of sharing knowledge in a noisy world. As a result of understanding debasement, I finally invested in crypto. I may be late to that party, but it was nice for the penny to drop.

If we need to keep asking for external validation, maybe we need to take a little more time for the penny to drop. At some point we have to trust ourselves.

"How was I so confused that through your reflection of me, I could somehow be complete. I complete my own circle, I was already free."

#48:

If I'm honest I found every question challenging, perhaps that was the point of this experiment!

The anonymity gave me the courage to speak up, something that I have been frightened about for some time. Getting my bare truth out into the world sparked the rebel in me and I've been feeding that courage and curious side of my personality ever since.

I never joined for external validation, I signed up to this crazy experiment because I wanted to be amongst others who too had the gumption to throw themselves into something completely unknown.

Thank you faxers for your raw and honest perspectives. In a world that often rewards superficiality, Fax Club has renewed my faith in the power of genuine expression. It's taught me that real connection comes not from having it all figured out, but from being brave enough to share our messy, beautiful truths.

Question 52

What's your question?

After 52 weeks, this is the last question. Here goes.

What is the one question you would have asked everyone in Fax Club? And why?

#48:

What has it been like being a number and how did the anonymity of Fax Club affect your experience?

#22:

As we reflect on a year of exploring counterintuitive questions, I'd like to ask something that looks beyond careers and work-related purpose.

How much effort do you put into cultivating a connection to something larger than yourself; whether that's a sense of wonder, a higher being, the natural world, or simply a feeling of interconnectedness?

How do you nurture this connection in your life, and what does it bring to you?

#103:

Have we all been truly counterintuitive?

And by that, I mean, how truly counterintuitive can you be, without crossing lines / alienating yourself / being totally overlooked and misunderstood?

#03:

I'd love to know why you all joined Fax Club? What specifically about it appealed to you?

My reasons are perhaps a little unusual. Here's why:

Back in the early 90s my dad had to go to New York for a work project. He ended up getting stuck there for a period of time, the reasons for which are pretty hazy in my 7-year-old brain, but the gist of it was I knew he couldn't leave. I have two younger sisters and during that time, he would send us a fax once a week. Every week, the fax machine would whirr into action and we'd all crowd round and receive our faxes. As the oldest child, I'd get a proper letter, which I was always really proud of and the others got varying degrees of words, pictures, descriptions of New York, etc.

I still have all the faxes in a little plastic envelope (one of those ones with the string that winds round the top, you know the ones). Some are illegible - that paper was never meant to last - and lots don't make sense as sections were cut out as the fax paper jammed or a page got missed, but I can still remember the whole set-up: the sound, the grey fax machine on a little red metal filing cabinet, the light in the room, the excitement of the paper spilling onto the floor.

One day, my aunt came round. She turned to my youngest sister and asked: "Where's Daddy?" My sister pointed at the fax machine. My aunt called my dad the next day: "You'd better come home, your daughter thinks you're a fax machine."

So, maybe I've always been part of Fax Club.

The end... or the beginning?

Against all the odds, we're a group of strangers who compiled a book. And against even greater odds, you're reading it. Welcome to the most inclusive exclusive club.

An experiment with no real plan, primarily organised over WhatsApp, with many individual and collective moments of, "Really?" and, "What actually is this?". But we all hung on.

Most of us have met each other once, some never. We live in the UK, the US, France, Portugal, Germany and The Netherlands.

We've tiptoed and stomped our way around leadership, ownership, personal stories, anonymity and abandonment. Asked ourselves why anyone would care, and asked ourselves: why did we?

The questions were interesting and challenging, in both their content, but also the commitment required to get to the end. However, what really kept everyone in was the experiment, the not knowing how or where it would end up. The connections and trust between people who have met each other once, or in some cases never, have really been something. We're now a community, one that's centred around an odd experience that's hard to explain in practical terms, but even harder to describe how it felt and feels. A community that's completed what it set out to do: answer some questions and produce a book.

We're also a community that's loyal, supportive, creative and resilient. Busy people who found time and energy to squeeze in something that both fulfilled them, but also helped each other.

How best to sum it up? Perhaps in the words of one of us on the day we all met for the first time:

"I don't know what it is, but would I do it again? Hell, yes."

About the authors

Identity and belonging drive much of human behaviour. We are given names when we're born and we take on more names as our identity grows and we find places of belonging. For an entire year we were an anonymous community known to each other only as numbers.

We are the Fax Club 32...

Judy Andrews, Rik Arron, Louise Barnard, Sally Bartlett, Jonathan Berry, Abbi Buszard, Christabel Cairns, Augustin Courau, Ben Davies, Iona Evans, Mariken Gaanderse, Claire Gillespie, Ellie Good, Ginger Grey, Adam Holloway, Sajni Lakhani, Simon Lodge, John Lunn, Rona Mackenzie, David Maris, Laura-Jane Marris, Ant Parsons, Karen Perry, Grace Rodgers, Charlie Simpson, Duncan Skelton, Nick Stoop, Anna Svitak, Natalia Talkowska, Patrick Ubezio, Hannah Verrall, Olly Whitman.

If wrestling with important problems and repeatedly *doing* things differently isn't getting the results you want, you need to step back and ask, "How might I *think* about this differently?"

Fax Club spent a year thinking about things differently. We spent a year *being* differently.

We can help.

If you're stuck, or need a different perspective, and if you don't know where to look, then get in touch. The 32 can get you moving.

Email us at **the32@TheFaxClubExperiment.com**.

Acknowledgements

To give credit where credit is due, this all started in West Wales with David Hieatt, founder of The DO Lectures. None of this would have happened if, in late December 2023, he hadn't put the call out for 100 strangers to buy a fax machine, and then patiently wait for it to whirr into action every Friday night and dutifully spurt out a question. For a year.

Over the following year of faxing, one person's efforts in particular kept things going. Claire Perry-Louise made sure a question was transmitted over the wires every Friday night and managed the technological challenges and changes as we were swapped from one online forum to another. At the end of the year, it was Claire who masterfully led a day that is, to date, the only time most of us have ever met in person.

That created 52 questions, a huge pool of answers, and a loosely connected group of strangers. But, that does not make a book.

This book exists due to the extraordinary efforts of a group of people better known as #03, #05, #06, #12, #13, #14, #15, #18, #22, #24, #25, #26, #32, #38, #42, #47, #48, #50, #71, #73, #74, #78, #79, #80, #85, #88, #89, #95, #98, #101, #102 and #103, with additional content from #11, #20 and #49.

The very definition of a group project, this endeavour had no blueprint. The group itself, whilst individually very talented, was an unknown quantity, with no specifically recruited skills or publishing experience. For the first few months, we fumbled along. Held together by this strange experiment and our commitment to do what we set out to do, but perhaps most importantly building a bond between us all as we went.

As with any group, skills and preferences emerged and certain people should be recognised for their specific contributions:

First came the organising and gathering: Ant made sure we met online, and kept meeting, most clearly demonstrated by our inability to meet independently the week he went on holiday. Those meetings started as tentative chats and over time became more and more detailed and productive. Ant and Christabel made sure the outcomes of those meet-ups were shared with the wider group to keep everyone connected and momentum flowing. KP and Sally surveyed us all on what it was like to take part and why we did it, and Ginger skillfully turned those comments into the 'Meet the members' sections. Grace and Anna explored our publishing options and Ant researched the ins and outs of shared authorship and ownership for 32 authors of one publication. Iona, Nick, and David regularly supported in meetings.

Then came the book's content and look-and-feel: Christabel kickstarted a mass team editing process that everyone got involved in, breaking up into pairs to wade through all the answers and pick favourites. Hannah set up impressive cross-checking spreadsheets to make sure everyone's voice was heard. Rona, Laura-Jane, John and Duncan proofread the entire initial manuscript. Ellie, Judy and Grace came up with original design concepts for the book and Grace worked on cover designs. John arranged the foreword, and Duncan and Christabel wrote introductions and endings. Hannah, Christabel, and Claire spent many evenings and weekends working on the final book's layout and edit, with support from Duncan and Laura-Jane, and Hannah took on the herculean task of actioning all our collective feedback.

And finally, with a finished book in sight: Duncan took to the stage at the 2025 The DO Lectures to give this book its first public voice. Duncan is responsible for our website and taking on the task of bringing other people along for The Fax Club Experiment journey (visit: thefaxclubexperiment.com to find out more). Ant got us organised in a financial sense and Claire, Anna and Duncan are leading the way on where we take this next and how to get this book out into the wider world, supported in their plotting by Abbi, Iona, Christabel and Hannah.

Not everyone in the group had the capacity to dedicate the time they wanted to during the book making stage, but that doesn't mean they were any less supportive from the sidelines and won't find the moment to promote this book in the future. If you see a lone stranger sitting with a fax machine in the middle of Manchester, or find a copy of this book with a note inside in an improbable place in the future, that may well be one of us. To those people: thank you for your cheerleading and original words, you were an integral part of the process.

Finally to the families, partners, friends, housemates and colleagues of those in Fax Club. Some of you knew about this from the beginning (a flagrant disregard for the rules, but we'll let that slide) and some of you may only be finding out about it now. Either way, you enabled us - whether knowingly or not - to spend some time thinking slowly, you tolerated our eccentricities, probably raised an eyebrow or two when we told you what we were up to and, most of all, gave us the space to meet some fantastic people and create something we can all be proud of.

So next time you're on a train, or in a café, or waiting in a queue at the post office, imagine what all the other people could tell you, the help you could give each other, the questions you could ask and the answers you could give, if only we all allowed ourselves the time and were brave enough to ask.

Find out what's next at:

TheFaxClubExperiment.com

Printed in Dunstable, United Kingdom

77278262R00117